FOR CLUB
AND
COUNTRY

FOR CLUB AND COUNTRY

THE BEST OF THE GUARDIAN'S

FOOTBALLING OBITUARIES

BRIAN GLANVILLE

guardianbooks

Published by Guardian Books 2008

2 4 6 8 10 9 7 5 3 1

First published in Great Britain in 2008 by
Guardian Books
119 Farringdon Road
London EC1R 3ER

A CIP catalogue for this book is available from the British Library

ISBN: 978-0-85265-107-0

Typeset by seagulls.net
Printed in Great Britain by CPI UK

Contents

Foreword

Footballers, unlike old soldiers, do not fade away. When a famous footballer dies, the lasting image will always be youthful and invigorating, as if he had played his last game only a few days earlier. Footballers long gone live on in film and video recollections. In that sense they are always with us.

Brian Glanville's obituaries do much to preserve this imagery. As an erudite, entertaining observer of the game for more than half a century he consistently recalls to life those who have enthralled countless thousands of football fans as well as filling column after column in the sports pages. Glanville's staggering memory has not only documented the basic career details but also, crucially, supplied those anecdotal asides that add a human touch to the facts and the feats. The 80-odd players remembered in this book offer an accurate reflection of the way football has been played over the last 60 years or more at home and abroad.

One of Glanville's strengths is his wide knowledge of the game overseas, which is evident in his recollections of such names as Helenio Herrera, Silvio Piola, Ladislao Kubala, Nandor Hidegkuti and many others.

Hidegkuti was a member of the Hungarian team that exploded the myth of English supremacy by winning 6-3 at Wembley on a murky November afternoon in 1953. Coronation year had witnessed one sporting triumph after another: Stanley Matthews had at last collected an FA Cup winners' medal, Gordon Richards had at last won the Derby and England the Ashes. When Hungary, the Olympic champions, threatened to end England's record of never losing to a foreign team at Wembley, some leading pundits of the day sniffed their doubts. Yes, yes, Hungary played nice football but like all Continentals they could not shoot to save their lives. England would win 3-0, that was the popular prognostication.

Hidegkuti took all of 90 seconds to disprove the notion that Hungary could not finish. After that, for England, it quickly became a matter of damage limitation. Ferenc Puskas, Hungary's captain who was also a major in their army, had given Wembley a foretaste with an ominously impudent piece of ball trickery before the kick-off. As Glanville recalls, Puskas had taught himself ball control by juggling with a tennis ball. In this game he scored twice, most memorably after dragging the ball back from Billy Wright's lunge before turning to shoot past Gil Merrick. Wright was left lunging at thin air. 'Like a fire engine going to the wrong fire' was how The Times's Geoffrey Green described it.

Puskas and his team brought home to England, the Football Association and the nation at large just how far behind Europe, not to mention South America, the domestic game had fallen. For Ron Greenwood and other young English coaches the Hungarians demonstrated, as well as their superior technique, the importance of players moving intelligently off the ball. At that time English football was still standing around when not involved in the imme-diate action.

It was surely no coincidence that one of the better English performances against Hungary that day came from Stanley Matthews who, at 38, was the oldest player in the side. Matthews, as Glanville writes, was 'arguably the outstanding English player of his generation'. Certainly he was the only member of that England team who would not have been out of place in the opposition. Yet for years arguments raged about whether Matthews should be picked for England when Tom Finney, the other outstanding English winger of the post-war era, was more direct and scored more goals — 30 in internationals compared with three from Matthews.

In those days the England team was selected by an international committee of butchers, bakers and candlestick makers who tended to advance the claims of players from their own clubs. Glanville recalls that in Matthews' early days in the 1930s there were those who doubted his temperament for important matches. He was regarded as too much of an individualist and, as Glanville points out: 'Over the years he would time and again fall foul of the England selectors.'

Happily the talent of the man prevailed enough times to bring England some famous pre-war victories when he was approaching his international peak. These included the 6-3 rout of Adolf Hitler's Germany in Berlin in 1939 after the England players had been prevailed upon to give the Nazi salute when the teams lined up for the national anthems. In fact Hitler was not at the match, being represented by Hermann Goering. At one point the British ambassador, Sir Neville Henderson, who had turned up wearing a shooting hat and an old pullover, offered Goering his binoculars so he could get a better view of the goals. The Reichsmarschall was not amused.

In the FA Cup final of 1953 Matthews enjoyed his crowning moment as a Blackpool player when he inspired the extraordinary recovery which saw Blackpool beat Bolton Wanderers 4-3 with virtually the last kick of the match after lagging 3-1 with 20 minutes to go. As Glanville recalls: 'It was now that Matthews, strangely obscure till then, at last came into the game.'

The truth was that up to this point Matthews had been a peripheral figure. He started to influence the match only when

Ernie Taylor began feeding him the ball through gaps left by the injury that had forced Bolton's Eric Bell, a midfielder, to limp along up front, a regular ploy in the days before substitutes. Bell scored Bolton's third goal but their legs, worn out through playing virtually a man short, could not cope with Matthews as he tormented their defence with that body swerve and sudden acceleration which plagued full-backs over four decades.

The 1953 final is rightly celebrated as the most dramatic of all time but, if the overall quality of the football seemed uneven and error-strewn at the time, it looks positively prehistoric now. The Hungary experience — as much the 7-1 defeat England suffered in Budapest in 1954 as the earlier humiliation at Wembley — bred a new generation of coaches and eventually persuaded the FA that England might benefit from a manager from the professional game who would choose his own players. This turned out to be a steady, slightly staid former Tottenham and England right-back who, as Glanville reveals, originally had it in mind to become a grocer.

Certainly Alf Ramsey was the unlikeliest of heroes. Originally a centre-forward for Southampton when he played for them as an amateur, he was switched to full-back and at White Hart Lane became one of the most reliable defenders in the land as he helped Tottenham win promotion from the Second Division in 1950 followed by the League Championship the following season. That Spurs team gave its First Division contemporaries a hint of the way the wind was blowing in the game since Arthur Rowe's push-and-run style — 'Make it simple, make it quick' — was, in terms of passing and movement along with an intuitive interchanging of positions, a forerunner of the football that humbled England in 1953.

Before becoming England manager towards the end of 1962 Ramsey had brought modest Ipswich Town up from the Second

Division to win the title a year later. Perhaps his ability to get the best out of slender resources, and the imagination he had shown in converting Jimmy Leadbetter, a wispy Scottish winger, into an astute playmaker for Ray Crawford and Ted Phillips helped to persuade the FA that here was the man to win the World Cup England were to host in 1966.

Not that Ramsey's international resources were as lean as those faced by more recent England managers. Even so the way Ramsey husbanded those resources was crucial to England's only triumph in a major international tournament. He eventually dispensed with orthodox wingers and withdrew Bobby Charlton, Leadbetter-fashion, from the left wing to play in the hole behind the strikers while using the youthful stamina and expertise of Martin Peters and Alan Ball to work the flanks.

Few managers have enjoyed as much devotion from their players as Ramsey received from his England squad. Brian Clough, an inspired iconoclast who was one of Ramsey's fiercest critics during his latter days with England, was equally adept in his ability to inspire footballers, often finding in them talents that they themselves were not aware they possessed. Yet Clough was totally different. As Glanville notes: 'Clough's methods were unique. He was essentially a dictator and not always a benevolent one.' Like Ramsey he won the league with teams recently promoted, Derby County and Nottingham Forest. Unhappily the FA was never brave enough to give him the England job. It might not have worked out but it would have been immense fun while it lasted.

Much the same may be said of the career of George Best who, like Clough, was eventually consumed by drink. 'Best,' says Glanville, 'was arguably the finest player produced in Britain since the war' and it would be hard to argue otherwise. It was difficult to equate the haggard, hollow-eyed figure of his last years with the wonderful young Ulsterman who had brought a new dimension to the game, on and off the field, in the 1960s. He was a bridge between the stars of today's celebrity game and Glanville's characters here. This book remembers Best at his best. That's what it's all about.

David Lacey

A note on the text

These 87 obituaries span the dozen years from 1996. Inevitably there is overlap. Rough contemporaries in death were naturally in some cases contemporaries in the game. Careers crossed in clubs or competitions, in great moments or matches. The obituaries stand corrected but otherwise as published. They could have run as a chronological hotchpotch. For ease of access they are chaptered – and alphabetical therein – while recognising that some could have qualified for other chapters, too. Brian Glanville has always enjoyed the big picture – Europe, especially Italy, and South America. An Arsenal XI betrays his true love.

1

Strike Force

Strike Force

Potter supreme

RONNIE ALLEN

Ronnie Allen, who has died aged 72, played for West Bromwich Albion from 1950 to 1961 and was one of the most talented and effective centre-forwards of his time. Yet he won only five caps for his country, a commentary less on his abilities than on selection policies.

It was especially bewildering that he should play no part in the 1954 World Cup in Switzerland. The previous April he and his incisive foil, Johnny Nicholls, had each scored in the 4-2 defeat of Scotland at Hampden Park. Allen had then scored twice to enable West Bromwich to beat Preston North End in the 1954 FA Cup final. A few months later he excelled in one of the most talented forward lines ever to play for England – another Wembley occasion when he scored in England's 3-1 victory over a depleted West Germany.

An ebullient Midlander, born in Fenton in the Potteries, Allen would jokingly say, 'Got to get the ball in the old onion bag' – and how often he did. Never a giant, standing but 5ft 8in tall and weighing barely 11 stone, he clearly did not fit the pattern of the dreadnought centre-forward long favoured in the English game.

In 1946 Port Vale, of the Third Division North, became his first club. There he emerged as an outside-right, playing during his national service for the Royal Air Force representative team. In 1950 he was transferred to West Brom for £15,000, a large fee for the time, and it was at The Hawthorns that he was converted into a centre-forward. He relied not on physique but on his skill, flair and speed of both movement and thought. He, and the whole team, undoubtedly benefited from the coaching of Jesse Carver in 1952, who put what was then an unusual emphasis on training with the ball before he returned to Italy to resume his career with Torino.

Above all Allen struck up the perfect partnership with Nicholls, a blond inside-left renowned as a goal poacher. Many of those goals were made for him by Allen, who was as adept with the short pass as he was with the long. Nicholls would time his runs perfectly to exploit, with his pace and power, the through-balls provided by Allen.

The 1954 Cup final saw Allen supreme. Preston had got ahead with what might easily have proved a traumatising goal, being plainly off-side, before West Brom, inspired by Allen and his two goals, came back to win the game 3-2.

The celebrated match against West Germany, again at the Empire Stadium, saw Allen leading an attack in which the wingers were Stanley Matthews and Tom Finney, the inside-forwards Roy Bentley and Len Shackleton. Alas, it was too good to be true and England soon returned to more conventional methods.

Allen's first international cap had come against Switzerland in 1952, his last against Wales in 1954. The mid-1960s saw him playing out his career with Crystal Palace, in the Second and Third Divisions. As a manager he began in 1965 with Wolverhampton Wanderers, winning them promotion to the First Division in 1967. The following year he went on to Athletic Bilbao (Atlético as it was then), winning the 1969 Spanish Cup, and later Sporting Lisbon.

Back in England in 1973 he briefly managed Walsall and later had two short spells as manager of West Brom, first in 1977, then in 1981-82, but with less success than he achieved as a player. His autobiography, *It's Goals That Count*, was published in 1955. Allen is survived by his second wife, Cynthia, to whom he was married for 30 years.

Ronnie Allen, born January 15 1929, died June 9 2001

JANUARY 21 2002

Hit-and-miss humorist

JEFF ASTLE

The centre-forward Jeff Astle, who has died suddenly aged 59 after collapsing at his daughter's home, was famously remembered for an important goal and a cataclysmic miss. The first came less than three minutes into extra-time at Wembley and won the 1968 FA Cup final for West Bromwich Albion against Everton. The second was two years later in Guadalajara, when he blazed an easy chance past the Brazilian goal in the World Cup, denying England an equaliser. 'How did Jeff miss that chance?' agonised Alan Ball by the pool next morning at the Guadalajara Hilton.

Capped five times for England, once as a substitute, Astle had turned professional at 17 with his local team, Notts County. Standing short of 6ft and weighing 11st 7lb, he was hardly a giant, though he was celebrated for his heading abilities.

West Bromwich took him from the Third Division to the First in 1964 and he went on to score 137 times for them in 292 games.

Much the most celebrated of his goals was that which won the 1968 final. Faced with a robust Everton defence, marked by a centre-back, Brian Labone, who would be a team-mate in the 1970 World Cup, and without a fellow striker, Astle spent much of the game working on the wings. He might have scored soon after half-time when, for once eluding Labone, he sent in a powerful header from Bobby Hope's cross that flew just wide of a post. His winning goal came when, stumbling through a possible foul by Howard Kendall, Astle raced on for a right-footed shot, which was blocked. When the ball came back to him, a fine left-footed drive tore past the Everton keeper, Gordon West, and into the top right corner of the goal.

In Guadalajara he came on against Brazil, eventual winners of the World Cup, as a substitute, with England a goal down. He immediately began to trouble a none too solid defence with his power in the air. Heading down a high cross, he gave Ball a clear opportunity but Ball threw it away. Later, when a panic-stricken Brazilian defender headed the ball to Astle's feet, he shot past a gaping goal.

Astle was first capped for England against Wales in 1968. His next four international appearances came the following season, against Scotland, Portugal and in the 1970 World Cup against Brazil and Czechoslovakia.

Astle was well known for his wry sense of humour and from 1995 he appeared on Baddiel and Skinner's Fantasy Football League television show. Off screen his speciality was imaginary postcards, which he would suddenly declaim. Arriving in Rio airport with the English party in 1969, he came up with this, supposedly from the England trainer Harold Shepherdson: 'Dear mother – No injuries yet, so I've not been seen on television. PS: Have still not carried a bag. Love Harold.' Astle later worked as a window cleaner with a sign 'Misses no corners'.

Jeff Astle, born May 13 1942, died January 19 2002

FEBRUARY 23 2004

Gentle giant

JOHN CHARLES

John Charles, the 'Gentle Giant' who has died in hospital from cancer aged 72, was one of the greatest British footballers of his era, a star in particular with Leeds United and Juventus. A precocious centre-half, capped for Wales while still a teenager, he subsequently became famous as a centre-forward, a compound of power, acceleration, heading ability and technique.

Born in Swansea, Charles was naturally apprenticed to Swansea Town, as the club was until 1970. But Major Frank Buckley, then manager of Leeds, heard of his prowess and lured him away. By early 1949 Charles had established himself as their dominating centre-half. The next March he won his first cap for Wales at 18, against Northern Ireland at Wrexham.

It was a disappointing debut. Charles was plainly nervous and for some time he lost his place to another gifted young centre-half, Ray Daniel, of Arsenal. Outwitted in that first international by the veteran Irish centre-forward Dave Walsh, of Aston Villa, Charles's massive physique, 6ft 2in and 15st, availed him little that day. He did get another chance at centre-half the following year but that, too, proved a difficult game against the Swiss. Wales scraped through 3-2 after building a 3-0 lead.

The turning point in Charles's career, which eventually took him to Italy and the adulation of Juventus fans, came when, in the 1952-53 season, Buckley decided to switch him to centre-forward at a time when the Leeds team badly needed goals. They got them. Charles scored 26 in the league.

Wales brought him back again, this time as partner to their forceful centre-forward, Trevor Ford. Northern Ireland were again the opposition, Wales won 3-2 and Charles was involved in all three goals. A left-foot volley scored the first one, a fine header the second and he made the pass for the third.

Both Leeds and Wales now shuffled him around in different positions. In 1955-56 his 30 goals in 41 games enabled Leeds to gain promotion to the First Division. Any doubts that Charles would be as formidable in the top division did not last long. He banged in 38 goals in 40 games.

British players in the highly competitive, highly rewarded Italian Serie A had long been a rarity but in the summer of 1957 the Italian players' agent, Gigi Peronace, took Charles to Juventus, the aristocrats of Italian football, the most popular club in the peninsula outside their native Turin, known as La Signora d'Italia. There Charles came under the benign patronage of the Agnelli family, who, in later years, when things went wrong, came to his financial rescue.

Flanked on one side by the Italian captain Giampiero Boniperti, on the other by the mischievous brilliance of the little Argentinian, Omar Enrique Sivori, another new signing, Charles flourished immediately. The Juventus fans adored him, nicknaming him Il Buon Gigante. He even recorded, with some success, the song, Sixteen Tons. His transfer had cost the then huge sum of £65,000, though Sivori had cost more. Despite the close, often illicit, attentions of Italian defenders, the nudging, shirt-tugging and obstruction, Charles maintained his placid, long-suffering demeanour. Once, when especially harshly treated, he is said to have turned to Boniperti and pleaded: 'You do something to them, Boni, I can't.'

That season Juventus won the Italian Championship and at the end of it John went off to join his brother, Mel, himself a notable centre-half, to play for Wales in the 1958 World Cup in Sweden. Had he not been viciously treated and injured by the Hungarian team in a sulphurous group play-off, who knows whether Brazil would have reached the semi-finals, let alone have won that tournament? John was unable to play in the quarter-final in Gothenburg. Inspired by the bravery of Mel and the goalkeeping of Jack Kelsey, Wales kept Brazil at bay for most of the game and even the solitary, decisive goal by Pele was a fluke, in off the boot of the Welsh right-back, Stuart Williams.

Initially the Welsh team found it hard to play to Charles, almost as if they were overawed. Against a Hungarian team that was a pale parody of the mighty side that should have won the 1954 World Cup Charles was chopped down three times in the first 16 minutes. He managed to score the equaliser, only for the Hungarians to be Wales's opponents in that play-off in Stockholm.

Here Charles was more brutally treated still, with no protection from a notorious Russian referee, Nikolay Latychev. At corners Charles found his arms pinioned by one opponent while another crashed into him from behind. He did not once retaliate. Indeed, the only known occasion on which he did was in a match against Austria when his brother Mel was carried off on a stretcher after a particularly vicious foul.

Wales again went a goal down and Charles, repeatedly hacked yet again, had to go off for treatment. There were no substitutes then. Charles limped back, put over a cross and Ivor Allchurch volleyed the equaliser. Later, exploiting defensive confusion, the Welsh right-winger, Terry Medwin, scored the winner. So Wales, who had qualified only because they had been given a second chance in a lucky-draw qualifying play-off against Israel, had reached the quarter-finals. In all Charles won 38 caps for his country and scored 15 goals.

In Italy he continued to be prolific. Playing all 34 games in his second season, as he had before and would again, he scored 19 goals in the championship. Twenty-three goals followed the next season, 15 in the one after. But by 1961-62 Charles seemed to be running out of steam. He scored only eight goals in 21 appearances in Serie A and the following summer Juventus transferred him back to Leeds. But even that last season in Turin had its peaks, notably Charles's performance at right-half in a European Cup game in the Bernabéu Stadium, where Real Madrid were beaten at home for the first time in European competition.

Charles's years in Italy had had their disappointments such as the end of his marriage to his first wife, Peggy, who at one stage decamped with a bathing attendant. Life for the wives of Italian club footballers could be hard, with their husbands away training.

Returning to Leeds was something of a disappointment. Charles played only 11 games for three goals before going back to Italy this time to Rome. For Roma he played 10 games, scoring four goals, but it was plain that the Italian romance was over.

Nine months later he was back, anticlimactically, in Wales to play for Cardiff City. He made 61 League appearances in his initial two seasons, scoring 11 times in the first but only three in the second. The third was depressing – eight appearances for a mere four goals. So Charles moved outside the league, eventually as player-manager for Hereford United. His immense, endearing cheerfulness was unimpaired but the spark had gone out of his game.

His remarkable power in the air remained and, though his managerial style was, to say the least, eccentric, there were moments of success. Joining the Southern League club in 1966, simply as a player, he scored 37 goals in 54 games in his first season. When Bob Dennison left the club in December 1967, the player-manager's dual role went to Charles. Hereford parted company with him in the 1971-72 season and in December 1972 he joined another Southern League side, Merthyr Tydfil, again as player-manager.

There he remained, in difficult economic circumstances, until 1974, when he returned to his boyhood club, Swansea, as youth team manager. He left the job in the summer of 1976, when Harry Gregg, club manager, former Northern Ireland keeper and an old friend, resigned. There was a four-month spell as technical director of Canada's Hamilton Steelers. Then he was home again.

For a time he ran a hotel in the north of England but that was unsuccessful. He was a hopeless businessman and his attempts to run a sports shop and two pubs ended in disaster and pursuit for unpaid rates. However, in Italy he was still King John, lionised and lauded whenever he made one of his frequent returns. He was awarded the CBE in 2001.

By his marriage to Peggy he had four sons. He married Glenda Vero in 1987 and she survives him.

William John Charles, born December 27 1931, died February 21 2004

MARCH 6 2008

Sheffield stalwart

DEREK DOOLEY

The short, prolific but doomed career of Derek Dooley, who has died aged 78, came to an abrupt end in a league match at Preston on February 14 1953. The Sheffield Wednesday centre-forward collided with the advancing goalkeeper, broke his right leg and, after weeks in hospital, had to have it amputated after gangrene set in. The red-headed Dooley, at 6ft 2in and weighing 13st 7lb, had already scored 16 goals for Wednesday in his first season in the First Division. The previous season, in the Second Division, he had scored a phenomenal 46, enabling Wednesday to win promotion.

His style did not appeal to everyone and he was frequently booed when Wednesday played away. With his bulk, his huge feet, his ungainly movement, his abrasive approach and his perpetual harassing of goalkeepers, Dooley was always a controversial figure. Were he playing today, he would never be able to inflict such punishment on goalkeepers as they went for high balls, though some, such as West Ham's rugged Ernie Gregory, returned his attentions in kind. In one game at West Ham Dooley deliberately held Gregory on the ground, enabling a team-mate to score, but it was Dooley who came off the field with a torn shirt and studmarks on his chest after the return game at Hillsborough.

There was never any malice about him, any more than there would be recriminations or self-pity after his career was cut short. At Deepdale, the Preston North End ground, he was pursuing a long pass from the clever little Albert Quixall, knowing that the advancing goalkeeper, George Thompson, was more than likely to get there first. In the event Thompson crashed into Dooley just as he made contact with the ball, breaking the centre-forward's leg in two places.

He was about to be discharged after nine weeks in hospital when he jokingly asked a nurse to autograph his cast. Playfully she began to tickle his toes, noticed with alarm that there was no reaction, confirmed that he felt nothing and called a doctor. It transpired that gas gangrene had been moving up the leg, which had seemingly been infected through a cut sustained before the collision. When Dooley awoke from the consequent operation, it was to discover that his right leg had been amputated 'six inches from the top because the gangrene had already reached my knee joint and beyond'.

It was all the more traumatic since he had married his wife, Sylvia, the previous June and was still only 23. 'In my heart and mind,' wrote Dooley, 'I was still chasing the ball down the middle.' But his resilience would prove exceptional.

Dooley was the son of two factory workers and was brought up in the Pitsmoor area of Sheffield. His father, who worked in various manual jobs until he was 67, had once been offered a trial by Bradford City but could not take the time off work to attend.

Leaving school at 14, Dooley took a job with a firm manufacturing hearing aids and joined the local YMCA so he could play football for them, initially as a centre-half but ultimately finding his preferred position of centre-forward. Before he was 19 he had been signed as an amateur for Lincoln City, finding his way into the first team in the Third Division North. Towards the end of the 1946-47 season Wednesday persuaded him to turn part-time professional, though there was strong competition from Wolverhampton Wanderers.

Oddly as it turned out, he made his league debut for Wednesday on March 11 1950 – just before national service in the RAF – at home to Preston. It would be nearly a year before he would play again.

Following the career-ending collision Dooley's huge local popularity enabled the *Sheffield Telegraph* and *Star* to promote a shilling fund which raised £2,700. This would be dwarfed by his benefit match, the first to be played under floodlights at Hillsborough, between an International XI and a Sheffield team, when 55,000 spectators contributed £7,500.

Dooley worked for a while as a journalist, then was employed for eight years at a Sheffield bakery. Eventually he combined the job with looking after Wednesday's juniors. In 1962 Eric Taylor, the club's general manager, gave him the opportunity to run their new development fund. It was the beginning of a long and notable career in the administration of the two Sheffield clubs. He was made Wednesday's manager in February 1971 but late in 1973 a new board of directors abruptly dismissed him.

The local rivals, Sheffield United, came to the rescue of a shocked and embittered Dooley, who would not go back to watch a game at Hillsborough for 19 years. In November 1974 United made him their commercial manager. These would largely be years of turmoil for United, who sank as low as the Fourth Division, but Dooley survived them, becoming in due course a director and eventually in 1999 chairman of the club. There could hardly have been a more popular appointment and in 2003 he was awarded the MBE. In April 2006, with the club celebrating promotion to the Premier League, he resigned as chairman and became vice-president.

He is survived by Sylvia, his son Martin and daughter Suzanne.

Derek Dooley, born December 13 1929, died March 5 2008

JUNE 25 2007

From the Doog to the chair

DEREK DOUGAN

Had Derek Dougan been a few years older, who knows what Northern Ireland might have achieved in the finals of the 1958 World Cup in Sweden. To get there at all was an astonishing feat, knocking out Italy on the way. But a mature Dougan rather than the gangling 19-year-old might have made all the difference.

Dougan, who has died aged 69, was then the highly promising centre-forward for Portsmouth. He was not Northern Ireland's first choice but Billy Simpson, the Glasgow Rangers centre-forward, had pulled a muscle after five minutes' training in Sweden, leaving Dougan to lead the attack in the first game against the Czechs, which the Irish won 1-0. Tall, agile, technically adroit, making good use of his height in the air, Dougan did not disgrace himself that day.

His career in football, variously as player, chairman of the Professional Footballers' Association and chairman of Wolverhampton Wanderers, was at once successful and controversial. Fluent to a fault, humorous, alert and plausible, he made as many foes as friends. There was always something of the maverick, the impulsive opportunist, about him. In 1979 he said of the ebullient and contentious Scottish manager Tommy Docherty: 'If he survives at Derby, it will be a remarkable feat. But he won't do it through his gift for repartee or off-the-cuff insults.' Five years later Docherty was managing Wolves while Dougan was chairman. They were not wholly dissimilar.

Dougan never managed a club but played for many, beginning in 1954 with Distillery of Belfast, the city where he was born. His second season with Portsmouth saw him transferred to Blackburn Rovers where, as his physical strength increased, so did his prowess.

In his first full season, 1959-60, he helped Rovers to reach the FA Cup final, versus Wolves, which made him seem a bargain at £11,000. But on the day of the final, the Doog, as he was nicknamed, suddenly demanded a transfer. Blackburn, after losing their full back Dave Whelan with a broken leg, lost 3-0.

The 6ft 3in Dougan did not get his transfer until he had played another full season for Blackburn. He then signed for Aston Villa. Overall these were not happy days. 'When I arrived at Aston Villa,' he later wrote, 'it was like joining a Guards regiment. At first the atmosphere was overpowering. I was with a great club and it's not easy to live up to such greatness. At the same time I enjoyed the stimulus and the challenge. It wasn't until much later, after I had left Villa, that I realised the peril of leaning too much on tradition. Villa were so mesmerised by past glories that they could not see what was happening to them until it was too late. Tradition was romanticised – a fatal mistake.'

One might say Dougan was a 'new footballer' before that being was invented. The truth was that his form fell away at Villa Park to such an extent that, when he was transferred in 1963, it was humiliatingly to an obscure Third Division club, Peterborough United. There he languished for two seasons until he was rescued by Leicester City, who bought him for £25,000 in 1965. Rejuvenated, he regained his place in the Northern Ireland side. Then, at the tail end of 1966-67, Wolves bought him for double what Leicester had paid and he stayed a Wolves player until 1976.

He remained an enigma. How could so seemingly rational, objective and eloquent a footballer occasionally commit such fearful fouls? And once, late in 1969, in a match against Everton, he got himself suspended for eight games for swearing at a linesman.

With his fellow Wolves players, he was not, it was said, a popular figure. Where many found him persuasive and intelligent, others saw him as arrogant and opinionated. There was a significant moment in the warm-up before an FA Cup semi-final. Steve Kindon, then a young left-winger, later to make Dougan imitations the essence of his after-dinner speaking, drove in a shot which hit Dougan in the genitals and knocked him out. The other players, far from sympathising, stood around laughing.

Dougan always had ambitions that went beyond football and, with the help of a loyal lieutenant, he produced various books about the game, including a novel, *The Footballer* (1974), much of which appeared to recount his feud with the Wolves manager, Bill McGarry.

In 1982 Dougan became chairman of Wolves, by then in deep financial difficulty. 'This is your club now,' he told the fans. 'I love you all. I am going to come amongst you.' Eight years earlier he had written: 'One wonders what some businesses would be like if they were run on the same haphazard lines as most football clubs still are. The amateur director has been kicked out of most industrial boardrooms, but not in football.'

Alas, things quickly went wrong. The Asian businessmen of Allied Properties who had bought Wolves failed to revive them, leading John Bird, the leader of Wolverhampton council, to lament, after a 5-1 defeat by Watford in 1983: 'They have brought this town into disrepute, making Wolverhampton the butt of every comedian's jokes. We must have a talk as soon as possible to find out where Allied Properties' interests lie. On Saturday's performance it is not in football.'

So Dougan's chairmanship came to a premature and disappointing end. Smoke without fire? Perhaps but he remained, above all as a player, one of the most magnetic figures of his day. In December 2005 he was one of the coffin carriers at George Best's funeral. He was also a representative of the UK Independence party. He is survived by two sons.

Alexander Derek Dougan, born January 20 1938, died June 23 2007

MAY 31 2003

Model T striker

TREVOR FORD

A forceful centre-forward in the classic British tradition – a giver and taker of hard knocks – Trevor Ford, who has died aged 79, played 38 times for Wales in an international career that spanned 11 years and brought him 23 goals. He originally joined his home team, Swansea Town, as a full-back but by the 1945-46 season, Ford, solidly built but hardly a giant at 5ft 10in and 12st, had established himself as a dashing centre-forward. His first game for Wales was a 1946 victory international against Ireland.

Ford would not even see out a full league season with Swansea, though in the 1945-46 season he scored 41 of their 90 goals. After playing 16 Second Division games for nine goals in 1946-47 he fell out with the club and was transferred to Aston Villa. The *casus belli* was a disagreement over how and when he should train before an FA Cup tie. Villa paid what was the then hefty sum of £9,500 to acquire him.

Ford would gratefully recall how, on his arrival in Birmingham, he was welcomed by George Edwards, whose place he was taking as Edwards moved to the right wing. Edwards shook hands and said, 'Trevor, I would like to extend a personal welcome to you. You're just the penetrating type of leader Villa needs and, if there's anything I can do to help you make the grade, just say the word.'

Ford's father had been a motivating force. 'He sent me to work two hours a night, practising, hammering a tennis ball against the wall to get my control right. And to stop me being one-footed, he soaked an old leather football until it weighed a ton and made me wear a plimsoll on my good right foot. I kicked it only once with that foot.'

Ford had happy years at Villa Park. But in 1950 he lost form and was transferred to Sunderland. Fifty-eight goals in his first three seasons would seem to contradict the conventional wisdom that he was never content at Roker Park because of his bad relations with the maverick inside-left Len Shackleton. It was true that they never got on, true too that the malign Shackleton, nicknamed the Clown Prince of Soccer, would sometimes put a bias on the ball so that, when it reached Ford, it would spin away from him. But Ford stayed with Sunderland until the 1953-54 season when, after nine goals in a dozen games, he returned to Wales, this time with Cardiff City.

Ford was no respecter of goalkeepers. Many years later he advised his international successor John Hartson to shoulder-charge keepers, then apologise. Ford himself was accused in the autobiography of the former England goalkeeper Gil Merrick of maltreating goalkeepers on a regular basis. He went to his lawyers and procured an apology, damages and the withdrawal of the book, asserting that he had never been cautioned, let alone sent off.

At Cardiff Ford continued to score goals, 19 in his second full season and 13 in the next. Then he fell out with the manager, Trevor Morris, who wanted him to play inside-left. When he saw himself down for the position on the team sheet, Ford walked out of Ninian Park and was suspended. Relations were patched up, though, and he remained with the club until 1957, when he was suspended by the FA after confessing to receiving illicit payments while at Sunderland, in that age of the iniquitously meagre maximum wage.

He nonetheless sued and went off to play for PSV Eindhoven. Three years later he came back to Britain and saw out his career with Newport County before going into the garage business with the comedian Stan Stennett. Altogether he scored 177 league goals in 348 appearances. Married for more than 50 years, he is survived by his wife and two sons.

Trevor Ford, born October 1 1923, died May 29 2003

November 7 1996

Headers first

Tommy Lawton

Tommy Lawton, who has died aged 77, has long been regarded as one of the finest centre-forwards to have played for England, scoring 22 goals in 23 games. Had he been operative now he would have earned, and been transferred for, millions of pounds. Instead he played for the relative pittance earned by the professionals of his time and in his declining years even found himself hauled into court on charges of petty fraud – a pitiful anticlimax to a remarkable career.

Like Nat Lofthouse after him, Lawton was born in Bolton and attended Castle Hill School. If Lofthouse was playing wartime football for Bolton at 15, Lawton was leading the Burnley attack in the Football League at 16. But why did he not join Bolton Wanderers? He was, after all, the outstanding schoolboy footballer in the town, even if he never won a schoolboy cap for England. Walter Rowley, then Bolton's coach, did try to sign him as an amateur, after a spell when he had trained two nights a week at Burnden Park. But their concurrent offers, of 10 shillings a week for a clerk's job or seven and six as a butcher's roundsman, were unattractive.

Advised by his grandfather and a former schoolmaster, WH Horrocks, Lawton showed a penchant for Anfield, where he had been applauded in schoolboy games, and Liverpool. But Liverpool, though interested, failed to come up with a part-time job; Bury, when approached, did not bother to watch him; Sheffield Wednesday were ruled out when Lawton's mother did not want him to leave home; and Burnley became the lucky club.

In May 1935 the 15-year-old, with his mother and grandfather, moved to Burnley. He was coached by a hard taskmaster in Ray Bennion, who made him endlessly practise his shooting and heading, running round the field to pivot and strike all the Bs in the advertisement 'BURNLEY'S BEER IS BEST'.

On March 28 1936, aged 16, Lawton made his League debut for Burnley in the Second Division against Doncaster Rovers. It was a draw. In his second game, at Swansea, he scored twice, the first with one of those typical, towering headers. It used to be said of him, and there has even been scientific evidence to suggest it was more than legend, that he could actually hang in the air before a header.

Working hard under Bennion, he improved his left foot until it was almost as powerful a weapon as his right. But though he scored freely with either foot, it was for his heading ability that he was most renowned.

Meanwhile, still only 16, he was playing League cricket, too, for Burnley under the aegis of the famous West Indian fast bowler Manny Martindale. He even hit the fabled Learie Constantine for six.

Five foot 11 and powerfully built, Lawton began the following season for Burnley with a burst of goals, three in a single game against Tottenham. By this time his grandfather – a familiar tale in soccer – had become the groundsman at Burnley's Turf Moor stadium and it was to him that Lawton turned for advice when emissaries from Everton arrived on the last day of 1936. He was duly taken on to the Everton ground staff.

There the plan plainly was that he should take over from the veteran Dixie Dean, a fabulous header of the ball and scorer of 60 First Division goals in the 1927-28 season. When Lawton, newly arrived, took the tram to Goodison, its conductor recognised him and told him: 'You'll never be as good as Dean.' Dean himself was benign. 'Youngster,' he said, the moment he saw Lawton. 'You've come here to take my place. Anything I can do for you, I will.'

Lawton's debut for Everton came quickly but was not auspicious. Though he scored from a penalty, the team lost 6-2. His direct opponent was a future colleague in many England teams, the elegant Wolves centre-half Stanley Cullis.

Lawton was in and out of Everton's team that first season, though he did play and score in a memorable Cup replay in the fifth round at Tottenham, Spurs winning 4-3 after being 3-2 down. He had played inside-right to Dean. After two initial defeats at the start of 1937-38 he replaced him definitively. It was an indifferent season for Everton but they began the following one with six wins in a row and went on convincingly to win the Championship, Lawton scoring 28 goals. The following season, his last in the First Division for the club, he scored another 34 League goals in 38 games.

He won his first cap for England as a 19-year-old at Cardiff against Wales in October, 1938. Again, though he scored from a penalty, he was on the losing side. Wales won 4-2. Lawton stayed in the England team, scoring at Highbury in a 3-0 win against the Rest of Europe (when the Uruguayan centre-half Miguel Andreolo, playing in Serie A for Bologna, notoriously spat at the referee) and getting the winner against Scotland at Hampden the following April. Those were the Blue Riband games then and his header from a characteristic Stanley Matthews cross made it 2-1 for England.

When war came Lawton, like many British professional footballers, was allocated to the Army Physical Training Corps at Aldershot. There he played as a guest for the little local club, which was able to deploy a galaxy of stars such as Cullis and Lawton's two Everton colleagues, the England wing-halves Cliff Britton and Joe Mercer. Wartime international games were not officially recognised but England had a spectacular team at the time. Scotland were beaten time and again, not least in 1943 by 8-0 at Maine Road, when Lawton scored four.

Everton were frequently at odds with their stars and Lawton did not stay after the war. A dispute led to his surprise transfer to Chelsea in the autumn of 1945 for the huge sum of £11,500. Almost at once he found himself leading the attack and scoring in a remarkable 3-3 draw at Stamford Bridge against the legendary Moscow Dynamo touring side.

When first-class football resumed he scored 26 First Division goals for Chelsea in 34 games. He continued to play for England and scored twice for Britain v Europe. But, still a restless figure, he demanded a transfer and, to general astonishment, moved to Notts County of the Third Division South for a British record fee of £20,000.

Meanwhile he had scored four times the previous May in a 10-0 win against Portugal in Lisbon, to which he added one of England's goals in a notable 4-0 win over Italy a year later in Turin in May, 1948.

Scoring freely, Lawton stayed with Notts County until the 1951-52 season, taking them up to the Second Division in 1949-50 with 31 goals in 37 games. He left Nottingham, where he had been involved with a firm selling typewriters, to become player manager of Brentford in the Second Division. Two seasons later he was brought back to the First Division by Arsenal, where he made 35 appearances for 13 goals.

For a while he was player manager of the non-League club Kettering. Next he went back to manage Notts County, nurturing the early careers of two young centre-forwards, Tony Hateley and Jeff Astle. But management was not his forte and his subsequent years in Nottingham were star-crossed, though he did, eventually, write with some success for the local paper.

Tommy Lawton, born October 6 1919, died November 6 1996

Peter Osgood

MAVERICK POWER AND FINESSE

The Chelsea, Southampton and England footballer Peter Osgood, who has died after a heart attack at a family funeral in Slough, aged 59, never truly fulfilled his enormous promise and potential. It was Geoff Hurst who scored three goals for England in the World Cup final of 1966 against West Germany, when Osgood was only 19. But, under a different manager from Alf Ramsey, the youngster, not even in the squad, might easily have played in his place. Precociously and richly gifted, an amalgam of power, finesse and opportunism, he had been in ebullient form that season in the Chelsea attack.

Osgood scored 150 goals altogether for Chelsea in 380 appearances but in his scintillating career played only four times for England, twice as substitute. Three of those caps came in the season of 1969-70 when he materially helped Chelsea win the FA Cup for the first time. Only the game against Belgium, his debut, saw him last the full 90 minutes. Osgood, with his dissident, sometimes rebellious character, was hardly the kind of player, whatever his possibilities, to appeal to the strait-laced Ramsey. Far less gifted contemporaries achieved far more international caps.

Osgood was born in Windsor and joined Chelsea as a junior in 1964. He missed their 1967 FA Cup final defeat by Tottenham, having broken his leg in the autumn of 1966 in a tackle with Blackpool's Emlyn Hughes, but he played a major role at centre-forward in their Cup success three years later, not least in the sixth-round 4-1 victory at Queens Park Rangers, when he scored three. There had never been a replay of the FA Cup final but after a draw against Leeds United at Wembley on an atrocious pitch, the clubs met again at Old Trafford. Leeds went ahead there but a spectacular goal from Osgood equalised and David Webb eventually scored the winner. Osgood is one of only nine players to have scored in every round of the Cup.

This victory put Chelsea into the European Cup-Winners' Cup, where they reached the final in Athens against Real Madrid. Osgood gave Chelsea the lead but Real equalised in the last minute. In the replay two days later on the same ground Osgood scored again, as did the Chelsea centre-half, John Dempsey, and this time the cup was Chelsea's.

Osgood was never likely to see eye to eye with Ramsey nor for that matter with his Chelsea manager Dave Sexton, a devotee of the Jesuit philosopher Teilhard de Chardin. Relations between Osgood, his friend Alan Hudson, a greatly talented young play-maker strongly influenced by Osgood himself, and Sexton came to the boil on Boxing Day 1973. Osgood and Hudson had been at odds with Sexton for some time. When they met West Ham United, Chelsea were 2-0 up at half time and seemingly well in command, only to collapse in the second half and lose 4-2, with Osgood and Hudson seemingly uninvolved.

A couple of games later Sexton dropped both men and soon afterwards, before another FA Cup tie at Queens Park Rangers, they refused to train with the first team. They were suspended, put on the transfer list and Osgood was sold to Southampton for £275,000. Sexton remarked: 'Maybe it would have been best if Ossie and I had sorted it out quickly between four walls of a locked room. But it wouldn't possibly have remained private with Ossie. He doesn't know when to be a good lad or Jack-the-lad.' Osgood got one more England cap that season against Italy but it would prove his last.

Standing almost 6ft 2in and weighing just under 12st, a compound of strength and technique, Osgood became one of a number of gifted veteran players who kept Southampton in the top division while Chelsea, without him and Hudson, were doomed to slide into the Second. He helped Southampton to a surprise FA Cup final victory over Manchester United in 1976 before joining the exodus to the North American Soccer League, but he was soon back at Chelsea, with Sexton having gone and former team-mate Eddie McCreadie now in charge. After his playing days he ran a pub in Windsor with another old team-mate, Ian Hutchinson.

On retiring Osgood became a match-day host at Stamford Bridge, only to cross swords with the always abrasive chairman, Ken Bates, and be brusquely banned from the stadium, though subsequently he was permitted to return. Latterly he was a well-known after-dinner speaker.

He was married three times and is survived by his wife, Lynn, and three sons.

Peter Osgood, born February 20 1947, died March 1 2006

DECEMBER 21 2002

Deadly with the left

ARTHUR ROWLEY

Arthur Rowley, who has died aged 76, had one of the most explosive left feet in post-war English football. Though he never quite achieved the stature of his older brother Jack, himself a formidable left-footed goalscorer for Manchester United and England, he was astonishingly prolific over many seasons. In all he scored 434 goals in 619 Football League games for four different clubs.

Born, like his brother, in Wolverhampton, he did not start at Wolves – where Jack was so quickly and rashly discarded – but West Bromwich Albion. Standing just under 6ft and weighing 13st 6lb, he was only a little better appreciated at The Hawthorns than was Jack at Molineux.

After a couple of league appearances in the first post-war season and 21 the next, for just four goals, he was sold early in the 1948-49 season to Fulham and at once flourished to such an extent that Albion could have rued the day they let him go. Rowley's 19 goals in only 22 games, from centre-forward, won Fulham the Second Division Championship, though Albion went up too, finishing a single point behind Fulham.

In the Second Division Rowley's left foot was a deadly weapon, from close or long range but the First Division was far less fruitful for him. He scored only eight times in his 34 matches, which suggests a gulf between his talents as a centre-forward and those of brother Jack, a regular scorer for Manchester United in the top division. Fulham seemed of that opinion too since, at the end of his second season at Craven Cottage, they transferred him to Leicester City, where he would stay for the next eight highly productive seasons. At Filbert Street the gulf narrowed for, when Rowley eventually returned to the First Division, he would be just as dangerous a striker as he had been in the Second.

His first four seasons at Filbert Street, in the Second Division, saw him score 115 goals, 30 of them in Leicester's 1953-54 promotion season, when they won the title on goal average from Everton. Back in the top division he then scored 23 times in 36 games, so it was hardly his fault that Leicester went straight down again.

In 1956-57, however, the club bounced back and this time there was no question of their doing it on goal average. With Rowley contributing another remarkable haul of 44 goals in 42 games, Leicester finished seven points ahead of their East Midland rivals Nottingham Forest.

Again Rowley did his bit in the top flight, with an honourable 20 goals in 25 games, and this time Leicester stayed up. At the end of the season, though, a still fully functional Arthur Rowley left them to become player-manager of Shrewsbury Town, arriving at a Gay Meadow that was anything but; the club had just finished 17th in the old Third Division South, having scored a parsimonious 49 goals, a placing that landed them in the newly formed Fourth Division.

Rowley soon changed all that. Banging away with that famous left foot, he scored 38 goals in 43 games, enabling the club to win promotion to the Third Division, no longer regionalised.

Though steadily gaining weight, Rowley continued to score prodigiously: 32, 28, 23 and 24 goals in the ensuing four seasons. Only then, in his last couple of years, did his strike rate fall away, with five goals in 1963-64, and two in a dozen games in his last season at Gay Meadow, 1964-65.

A short spell at Sheffield United, as joint manager with John Harris, the former Chelsea centre-half who had been at Bramall Lane for years, was ill-augured. Harris did not want anyone to share his authority and Rowley himself was known as a forceful, uncompromising, even perhaps authoritarian character.

He was much happier when, in 1970, he became manager, for the next six years, of Southend United. In 1971-72 Southend came second in the Fourth Division, though in 1975-76, Rowley's last season in charge, they returned where he found them.

He subsequently pursued a business career. His wife and son survive him.

Arthur Rowley, born April 21 1926, died December 19 2002

DECEMBER 31 2002

Taken as Red

ALBERT STUBBINS

On the sleeve of the Beatles' Sergeant Pepper's Lonely Hearts Club Band is the image of a footballer: Albert Stubbins in his Liverpool heyday, red shirt, red hair. He was a hero to thousands of Liverpool fans and, intriguingly, to fans of his original club, Newcastle United. Indeed, it might be said that Stubbins' fame has increased on Tyneside since his retirement long ago.

Stubbins, who has died aged 82, was a Geordie, born at Wallsend. His parents took him to the United States for two years just after his birth. They went back there at the beginning of the Depression and Stubbins spent a number of years in the US.

He trained as a draughtsman and at the start of his sports career he signed amateur forms for Sunderland but on the peculiar understanding that, if Newcastle United showed an interest in making him a professional, he could leave. This happened in April 1937 and he scored prolifically for Newcastle during the war, when official competitions were suspended.

Powerfully built, standing 5ft 11in and weighing 12st 10lb, he was his era's complete centre-forward: fast, strong, technically competent, adept at holding his line together, formidable in the air. In keeping with his genial character he never went selfishly in search of goals, though in those war years he was the country's top scorer. In the 1945-46 transitional season, before League football was restarted, he scored 39 goals in the Northern League for Newcastle. He was always robust but never unfair. The second-highest Newcastle scorer was a young outside-right called Jackie Milburn, with 14 goals.

Milburn, moving to centre-forward, would, as 'Wor Jackie', become a greater icon on Tyneside than Stubbins but many believe Stubbins was a still better centre-forward. Despite all Stubbins' goals, Newcastle finished only sixth in the Northern League that season.

It was also the season in which Stubbins made his only appearance for the English international team. It came in an ill-starred game on October 20 1945, against Wales at West Bromwich. The Welsh, famous for being able to rise above themselves, won 1-0. Stubbins never had another England chance and, since this was a so-called 'victory international', he never won a full cap.

In September 1946 Newcastle transferred him to Liverpool for £13,000. Playing alongside a shrewd inside-right in the form of Jack Balmer, he finished as joint top scorer in the league; they got 24 goals each as Liverpool narrowly and perhaps fortunately won the Championship when the season was prolonged by appalling winter weather. Wolverhampton Wanderers seemed to be running away with it but in their and Liverpool's last game at Molineux the visitors won 2-1, Stubbins scoring their second goal. The title was still open and, if Stoke City won their final game a fortnight later, they would win on goal average. But, though they had gone 11 league games undefeated, Stoke lost 2-1 at Sheffield United.

Stubbins continued to flourish in the 1947-48 season and Liverpool continued to count their lucky stars in getting him. He had asked Newcastle for a transfer and at least 18 clubs had made inquiries. Liverpool, using a recognised centre-half, Bill Jones, at centre-forward, had just been thrashed by Manchester United in an early 1946-47 league game when they beat all opposition to Stubbins' transfer.

After his 24 goals in 36 games when the league was won, he added another 26 in 40 matches the next season. Then something seemed to go wrong. He became unhappy at Anfield and asked for, but did not get, a transfer. He played five more seasons for Liverpool, yet scored only 27 more goals in the First Division.

He did help the club reach the 1950 FA Cup final against Arsenal, when he led the attack at Wembley, though not fully recovered from an injury, and Liverpool lost 2-0. The last of his first-team appearances was at Stoke on January 3 1953.

In 1960 he briefly became manager of the semi-professional New York Americans. He then returned to the north-east, where he became a popular sports writer. In the late 1990s the local branch of the Football Writers' Association gave him a gala dinner. He and his wife, Anne, had one son, Eric.

Albert Stubbins, born July 13 1920, died December 28 2002

2

An Arsenal XI

Made by Geordie

George Armstrong

The former Arsenal winger George Armstrong, one of the heroes of their famous 1971 League and Cup double side and latterly reserve team coach, has died suddenly after collapsing on the club's Hertfordshire training field, aged 56. He was Arsenal to the marrow, making 621 first-team appearances in a 15-year playing career, to be surpassed only by the present Leeds United manager, David O'Leary with 722,and now Tony Adams (624).

In an age when the traditional winger was due to disappear, 'Geordie' Armstrong, as he was always known, was the winger *par excellence*. Being two-footed, he was able to play on the right or left and was an unselfish creator of chances for other people with his accurate crosses. He was never a prolific scorer himself but reached 66 in his Highbury career.

Born in Hebburn, County Durham, he went to Highbury straight from school, discovered by Arsenal's north-eastern scout. He played his initial game for the first team in 1961 and 10 years later was a salient figure in the team that became only the second of the 20th century, after Tottenham, to win the FA Cup and League Double. That season he figured in every one of the 42 Championship games and was on the right wing at Wembley, the only real winger in the Arsenal side for the winning Cup final against Liverpool.

He was no giant, standing short of 5ft 7in and weighing just over 11 stone, but courage was never lacking – not when he was playing with the local Leslie's Boys Club nor in his long professional career.

Typically, in the Cup final, Armstrong popped up on either flank and very nearly scored when, on the far post, he surged in from the left to meet a right-wing cross from John Radford, only to be denied by a brilliant parry from Ray Clemence, the Liverpool goalkeeper.

In 1970 he had won a medal in the European Inter-Cities Fairs Cup and the following season scored one of the two goals whereby Arsenal, in the same competition, beat Lazio 2-0 at home. In 1972 he was on the losing Arsenal side in the FA Cup final against Leeds United. He also played in two losing League Cup finals, in 1968 and 1969.

In 1977 he left Arsenal to play for Leicester City and he finished his career at Stockport County. He then became a coach at various clubs, including Aston Villa and Fulham, and even managed the Kuwait national team. Almost inevitably, perhaps, he returned to Highbury, brought back in 1990 by his former team-mate George Graham, who said: 'He was such a thorough professional and a great help to me at Arsenal. As soon as I knew he was available when he was out in the Middle East I jumped at the chance to bring him back.'

Armstrong proved outstandingly successful at nurturing young talent. Ray Parlour, a current first-team player and England international, was one of his protégés in the reserve team, as was the Scottish striker Paul Dickov, who has gained honours this season with Scotland, as a Manchester City striker. The centre-backs Andy Linighan and future Northern Ireland international Stephen Morrow also came under his aegis.

Money meant little to him and he was critical of the attitude of many modern players. One who knew him well at Arsenal observed that 'football flowed out of him'. He was humorous, modest, unfailingly genial and survived the various changings of the guard at Highbury in recent years. He is survived by his wife, Marjorie, and their son and daughter.

George 'Geordie' Armstrong, born August 9 1944, died
November 1 2000

OCTOBER 8 2003

Borderline Englishman

JOE BAKER

Joe Baker, the former Arsenal, Hibernian, Nottingham Forest and
England centre-forward, who has died aged 63, could hardly have
been more Scottish, though born in Liverpool. The son of a sailor,
baby Joe was whisked back over the border to Wishaw, Lanarkshire,
when his father left the navy but his accident of birth was enough
for successive England managers, Walter Winterbottom and Alf
Ramsey, to pick him for the international team.

He played for them eight times, though to his disappointment
did not make the cut for the 1966 World Cup squad despite a lively
performance in December 1965 against Spain in Madrid where a
2-0 win was seen by some as the turning point in the fortunes of
a side destined to go on to win the World Cup. Baker scored
England's second goal, after a sweeping move, and kept his place
the following month for the 1-1 draw with Poland at Goodison
Park but thereafter Ramsey decided he would look elsewhere.

Baker played schools' and boys' football in Lanarkshire and won
a Scottish schoolboys' cap before joining Hibernian, where he
flourished. In his first season he scored all four goals in a 4-3 win
in the Scottish Cup against Hibs' Edinburgh rivals, Hearts, and
159 goals in four years.

He made his debut for England on November 18 1959, scoring

one of the goals in an unconvincing 2-1 win at Wembley against Northern Ireland, and kept his place for the rest of the season, playing against Scotland at Hampden and, on tour, against Yugoslavia, Spain and Hungary without further goals. There followed a hiatus until, almost five years later, he was recalled to the colours against Spain by which time he was playing for Arsenal.

Though small for a centre-forward, standing 5ft 7in and weighing 11st 9lb, he was fast, brave and tough, with good close control. He was also pretty handy, should occasion demand, with his fists.

Hibernian sold him to the Italian club Torino for £75,000 in 1961 after he demanded a £5-a-week pay rise on his current £12. During an unhappy season there he knocked an importunate paparazzo into a Venetian canal. On the field there was a later battle with the far taller, heavier Ron Yeats, Liverpool's centre-half, during a match at Highbury. To some surprise it was Yeats who was knocked down. Both players were sent off.

His move to Torino at the same time as the club signed Denis Law from Manchester City always seemed mistaken. Torino had never really recovered from the air crash of 1949, which wiped out the whole of their then dominant team. Fiorentina, by contrast, were a well supported and successful club and Baker subsequently admitted he would have been better off in Florence.

Baker and Law shared an apartment in Turin but never settled, though Law hugely impressed the Torino fans. Things came to a climax when, in the small hours of one morning in 1962, the two of them crashed their car in Turin. Not long afterwards both left, Law to Manchester United and Baker to Arsenal for £70,000, where he made 144 First Division appearances and scored 93 goals. In the FA Cup he scored in four out of 10 games.

In February 1966 the Gunners transferred him to Nottingham Forest, where he scored 16 league goals in each of two seasons. Subsequently he joined Sunderland, returned to Hibernian, moved to Raith Rovers, managed Albion Rovers and became a publican and club hospitality host at Hibernian. He is survived by his wife Sonia, daugher Nadia and son Colin.

Joseph Henry Baker, born August 17 1940, died October 6 2003

SEPTEMBER 29 1998

Cornish hopper

RAY BOWDEN

Ray Bowden, who has died aged 89, won six caps for England and outlived all his contemporaries from the all-conquering Arsenal teams of the inter-war years. An inside-right or centre-forward, he was born in Looe and was one of the relatively few players from Cornwall to make a major impact on the game, bringing to it his county's serene, untroubled approach.

Like his West Country team-mate in the Arsenal attack, Cliff Bastin, he was not eager or impressed when Herbert Chapman, Arsenal's fabled manager, came to sign him. He turned him down twice and was 25 by the time he moved to London whereas Bastin had been only 17.

Compactly built with dark, wavy hair, Bowden was an early perfectionist, with the habit of hopping on one leg all the way to school, then hopping all the way home on the other. The feat of scoring 10 goals in a game against Tavistock, when still only 15, brought him to the attention of Plymouth Argyle, whose officials persuaded him to sign for them in 1926. He was eventually chosen for the Third Division South league side.

Far from this causing unalloyed delight, Bowden later reflected that he had 'felt sorry about putting a married man out of a job', knowing it would signal the end of the road for the inside-forward he had replaced. 'I'll never forget the look on his face,' Bowden said.

He soon made an impact with Plymouth, a team that seemed constantly on the verge of promotion and finally managed it in 1930. The following year Bowden toured Canada with the Football Association party. Altogether he scored 83 goals for Plymouth Argyle.

Arsenal were looking urgently for a replacement for their illustrious inside-right, David Jack. Twice Bowden, happy in the West Country, turned down offers from Chapman – no easy decision when Arsenal were so dominant and Chapman so highly respected. But early in 1933 he finally moved to Highbury, making seven league appearances. The following season he would make 32 of the 42 games, with 24 in the season 1934-35. In all three Arsenal won the Championship.

His team-mate Bastin was never wholly persuaded of Bowden's virtues. In his autobiography he wrote that 'Ray was capable of being a great player on some days. On others he was very disappointing.'

Playing not only at inside-right but at times at inside-left and even centre-forward, Bowden won his first cap for England against Wales in the autumn of 1934. In November he was one of seven Arsenal men chosen to play against Italy, then holders of the World Cup, in the torrid Battle of Highbury.

Bowden, like Bastin, would later recall that he had not found the game as brutally rough as some other England players, notably the left-back Eddie Hapgood, who had his nose broken by an Italian elbow. 'Monti was taken off shortly after the kick-off with a broken toe and I think they lost their heads a bit,' Bowden remembered.

Luisito Monti, Italy's ruthless centre-half, in fact broke his toe in a clash with yet another Arsenal man, Ted Drake, and went off in agony claiming, 'He kicked me deliberately,' something Drake always denied. The Italians felt they were only 'retaliating'.

In 1936 an injury to Drake resulted in Bowden being moved to centre-forward, where he flourished in Arsenal's FA Cup run. In a tight semi-final against Grimsby Town at Huddersfield it was he who gave the pass from which Bastin shot the winning goal.

Despite Bastin's advice George Allison, Chapman's managerial successor, restored Drake to centre-forward for the final and he scored the winning goal against Sheffield United from Bastin's centre. Bastin, with his usual candour, recorded that Arsenal did not play well and were lucky to win while 'Ray Bowden was a failure at inside-right, really not his proper position, and was very seldom in the game. One can sympathise with him, as he had been leading the Arsenal attack for a considerable period and there is a vast amount of difference between the two positions.'

Bowden scored 43 goals in 143 games for Arsenal. Eventually he was transferred to Newcastle United and although, according to Bastin, he did not want to go, he later decided it was a fine club. He scored six goals for the north-east side. After retiring from football he returned to Plymouth to run a sports outfitters.

His wife predeceased him. His son and two grandchildren survive him.

Edwin Raymond Bowden, born September 13 1909, died September 23 1998

APRIL 24 1997

A law unto his sweep

DENIS COMPTON

Has there ever been a more brilliantly entertaining and magnetic all-round sportsman than Denis Charles Scott Compton? One who brought so much joy to both football and cricket, who disdained the banal and defensive, who so obviously enjoyed his sport?

Compton, who has died aged 78, was best known as a prolific batsman with an infinity of strokes but, had he lived at another time, he would surely have joined the select few officially honoured by England internationally at both cricket and soccer. The heart was torn out of his football career by the war, in which he served with the Army Physical Training Corps, much of the time in India where he excelled even at rugby.

His summer *mirabilis* at cricket was in 1947, shared appropriately with Bill Edrich, his Middlesex 'twin' and a talented outside-left with Tottenham Hotspur. Middlesex romped to the County Championship. The batting order of Sid Brown, Jack Robertson, Edrich and Compton built the bridgehead for victory after victory. Both Compton and Edrich topped 3,500 runs in the season, Compton ending with 3,816 runs and 18 centuries. Against the South African touring team he scored 753 runs, with four centuries and an average of 94.12.

Compton played soccer 11 times for England during the war, with a victory international against Scotland in 1946 to boot. But none of these counted as official caps. Outside-left was always his position from the moment he joined Arsenal from the Hampstead club (now Hendon) in 1935. He had a formidably powerful left foot and delighted in ball jugglery. One afternoon at Chelsea, not long back from India, he whimsically cushioned the ball a few times on his temple before hooking a perfect centre over his head into the goalmouth. 'Heads I Win, says Denis' read a Sunday paper headline next day. He had headed both goals in Arsenal's 2-1 win.

Compton's big brother, Leslie, had joined Arsenal three years before him but had to wait until 1946 for a regular place in their league team. Leslie, also picked for England in the war at full-back, did become a full international but not until 1950 and the age of 38, when he twice played centre-half for England.

Denis was born in north London. There was no special athletic tradition in the family but he was a prodigy, a Middlesex batsman and Arsenal First Division player at 18. He had barely passed that birthday when he made his debut for Middlesex against Sussex at Lord's at Whitsun, where he batted at No 11. He did not stay so low in the order for long. A few weeks later he made his first county century and enjoyed so successful a season that some thought he should have been a member of the Test party to tour Australia that winter.

Instead that September he made his league debut for Arsenal against Derby County, one of 14 appearances that season which produced four goals. When he and Leslie played blow football as boys, Leslie was always Arsenal while Denis was reluctantly obliged to call himself West Ham United. At Highbury the other players joked about his cricketing prowess. 'Well done, Denis,' they would say in the dressing-room at half-time, 'but you'd do even better in the second half if you took your pads off.'

Whether he was playing football or cricket, the essence of Compton's game was enjoyment, which he abundantly communicated. In both sports he was unorthodox to a degree, though never a fault. His unorthodoxy was underpinned by exceptional technique. George Allison, Arsenal's manager when Compton arrived, once cheerfully complained that when he gave Compton advice, Compton would solemnly reply, 'Yes, sir', then go out to do exactly what he wanted.

Batting, he delighted in scurrying down the wicket to attack even a good-length ball. The sweep to leg was a stroke he had honed to perfection. Where others might have run risks he regularly got runs. He was no less effective on the off side, where one of his specialities was to delay his shot before driving the ball square. Another feature was the way he dealt with off-breaks, taking a step back to strike the ball, daringly, against the spin. His on-driving was just as powerfully effective.

Unorthodoxy did once become controversy when, playing in a 1946 Test against India at The Oval, he ran out Vinoo Mankad by using his famed left foot to kick the ball on to the wicket.

Though a right-handed batsman, he was ambidextrous, bowling slow left arm in a variety of ways. Best known, perhaps, for his 'Chinaman', he could produce orthodox left-arm spin if required. His bowling was never in the same class as his batting, though when he struck a length it could be formidable. Altogether he took 622 first-class wickets at 32.27 and 25 Test wickets at 56.40. That last statistic may sound unimpressive but it includes a remarkable five for 70 against South Africa in Cape Town on the 1948-49 MCC tour. His best figures came on the 1946-47 MCC tour of New Zealand against Auckland, when he took seven for 36.

Looking at the statistics, it is curious that, though he made his debut for Arsenal so early and continued to play for them on and off until 1950, he made only 54 league appearances for a mere 15 goals. This is partly accounted for by the intervention of the war, during which he was a regular member of the Arsenal team until posted to India in 1944. He played in the team which won the

League South double of championship and cup, helping Arsenal to crush Charlton Athletic 7-1 in the final at Wembley.

Above all he was a member of a brilliant England forward line, made up of Stanley Matthews, Raich Carter, Tommy Lawton, Jimmy Hagan and himself, which would surely have excelled in peacetime football, too. It reached its peak when it overwhelmed Scotland 8-0 at Maine Road in 1943. Compton played a large part in that success and in numerous others.

He made a huge contribution also to Arsenal's winning of the FA Cup in 1950. He scored against Burnley, beaten 2-0 at Highbury, with a typically ferocious left-foot cross-shot and flourished at Wembley in the final against Liverpool. The story goes that he was feeling out of sorts at half-time and Alex James, formerly the hub of Arsenal's pre-war team at inside-left, gave him a glass of brandy to pep him up.

Another reason for Compton's relatively few post-war games for Arsenal – aside from the long winter cricket tours with MCC – was the protracted trouble he had with his right knee, which greatly affected his cricket, too. Arsenal certainly missed his left-wing trickery and especially his coolness from the penalty spot.

The knee inevitably cut down his effectiveness not only as a batsman but as a dashing fielder, though his coordination and athleticism still made him capable of sensational catches. The mind's eye sees him still at Lord's in 1942 playing for a combined Middlesex and Essex team against Kent and Surrey. Godfrey Evans, the celebrated Kent wicket-keeper and no mean batsman, pulled a ball high to the boundary. It seemed a certain six but Compton, with a tremendous turn of speed, pulled off a remarkable catch.

Compton made his Test debut in 1937 against New Zealand, scoring 65. The following year, when the Australians came to England, he played in four Tests and made 214 runs, with one century, averaging 42.80. He had three Tests and an average of 63, including a century, against the West Indies.

When he returned from India in 1946 Compton had put on a lot of weight and, though he played his victory international match against Scotland at Hampden, he would never be quite the same footballer again. Much more serious was the knee trouble which first afflicted him in the last match of his golden summer of 1947. Previously he had had a most successful 1946-47 Australian tour: 459 runs at 51, with a century in each innings in the Adelaide Test.

Alas, that knee would never leave him without pain and difficulty thereafter, though it did not stop him in 1948 scoring 145 not out at Old Trafford against Don Bradman's triumphant Australians even though at one point in his innings he was knocked out by a ball from Ray Lindwall and temporarily had to retire hurt.

The following winter he went on MCC's South African tour, making an astounding 300 in three hours at Benoni, but 1950 was a grim cricketing year. An operation to take a fragment of bone out of his knee meant he missed the bulk of it. The kneecap itself would be removed in November 1955 but, with typical resilience, Compton was still batting well enough to make a fine 94 against Australia the following year. Nor, among his brilliant innings of the 50s, should his 278 in four hours and 50 minutes against Pakistan at Trent Bridge in 1954 be forgotten. Compton played on until the end of the 1957 season, having appeared in 78 Tests, scoring 5,807 runs, with 17 centuries, for an average of 50.06. In first-class cricket he hit 123 centuries and nearly 39,000 runs.

For many years after the war his handsome face appeared all over Britain in the celebrated Brylcreem advertisements. On retirement he wrote a column for the *Sunday Express* and commented on BBC television.

As for his understanding with Leslie, when both played for

Arsenal, there was never a better example than in the 1950 FA Cup semi-final against Chelsea at White Hart Lane. Arsenal, a goal down near the end, were given a corner. Leslie came striding upfield from centre-half. Joe Mercer, Arsenal's captain, waved him back. Leslie ignored him, Denis put over the left-wing corner, Leslie headed the equaliser and Arsenal went on to win the Cup.

The understanding was not always so obvious on the cricket field. At Leslie's benefit match in 1955 Denis ran him out before he had faced a ball.

Denis Compton, born May 23 1918, died April 23 1997

AUGUST 26 1999

Mistaken for Matthews

ALF KIRCHEN

'From village boy to a lion of London!' exclaimed the *Topical Times* sporting annual for 1935. Alf Kirchen, who has died aged 85, had just joined Arsenal from Norwich City for a £6,000 fee. Born in Shouldham, Norfolk, he had been recommended by the Norwich manager, Tom Parker, formerly Arsenal's stalwart captain.

Kirchen had to wait another couple of years before replacing the incumbent outside-right, Joe Hulme.

He made a spectacular debut for the Gunners on March 6, 1935, scoring twice in a 6-0 win at Tottenham. Like Hulme he was unusually fast but he also had great power and could function successfully on either flank. Indeed he figured in both positions when capped three times on England's 1937 tour of Scandinavia. Having finally won a regular place in the Arsenal attack, Kirchen was awarded a Championship medal for the 1937-38 season, when he made 19 appearances.

When war came, like many Arsenal players, he joined the RAF. England would pick him three times more, once in 1942, against Scotland, in Glasgow. Chosen at outside-left, with Stanley Matthews on the right wing, Kirchen arrived at the Glasgow hotel where England were staying and politely greeted one of the selectors in the lobby.

'Who are you?' the selector inquired. 'You ought to know, sir,' rejoined Kirchen. 'You picked me to play on the wing.' 'Oh, yes,' said the selector. 'How are you, Matthews?'

Kirchen played regularly for the powerful RAF representative team and an Arsenal side that reached a peak in the 1943 League South Cup final by thrashing Charlton Athletic 7-1 at Wembley.

His career ended sadly and suddenly that year at West Ham after a collision severely damaged his knee ligaments. It was feared he might never walk again but a skilful operation saved him from being crippled. He had played 269 times for Arsenal, scoring 167 goals. He also represented England at clay-pigeon shooting.

Returning to his native Norfolk, Kirchen became a successful farmer and was eventually appointed a director of his first League club, Norwich City.

His wife, Vera, predeceased him but he leaves three daughters.

Alfred John Kirchen, born August 26 1913, died August 18 1999

FEBRUARY 21 1998

Back by persuasion

GEORGE MALE

George Male, who has died aged 87, once said to Arsenal's famous outside-left Cliff Bastin: 'By the time I came out of that room I was not only convinced I was a full-blown right-back, I knew without doubt that I was the best right-back in the country.' Which in the event he became.

The room was the office of Arsenal's manager, Herbert Chapman, who had almost legendary powers of persuasion. The time was autumn 1932. Male was a reserve wing-half of apparently moderate abilities. Chapman had decided that Arsenal's right-back and captain, the respected Tom Parker, had come to the end of the road. The apparent successor was Leslie Compton, brother of the great footballer-cricketer Denis, who had joined the club as a right-back the previous year. But Chapman decided Leslie was too slow. So Male got the job.

Born in East London, he had played senior amateur football in the Isthmian League for Clapton, joining Arsenal in 1930 and making his league debut at left-half that same year. The following season he played nine league games but his most important appearance was an unexpected one, in the FA Cup final of 1932. Arsenal were due to play Newcastle United at Wembley and Alex James, inside-left and fulcrum of their attack, was in doubt. The issue was settled when, in training at Brighton, Tom Whittaker, the Arsenal trainer, on Chapman's orders, subjected James to a powerful tackle. James collapsed in agony and Chapman, shuffling the team, brought in Male at left-half.

Things went wrong for Arsenal at Wembley when they succumbed to a notorious over-the-line goal. Jimmy Richardson pulled the ball back when it had crossed the byline and Jack Allen headed in. The goal was allowed and Arsenal lost 2-1.

Later that year Male was installed at right-back and stayed there with great success up to the Second World War, when he joined the Royal Air Force. He was a perfect complement to the rather more elegant left-back, Eddie Hapgood, who became captain of England, a position Male held later. They played together for their country 14 times as Male won 19 caps, the first in the torrid circumstances of the Battle of Highbury in November 1934, when England beat Italy. He had come in as a late replacement for the veteran Tom Cooper and was one of seven Arsenal men in that England team.

'George Male,' wrote Bastin in later years, 'perhaps lacked Eddie Hapgood's polish. He had a positional sense which was not a jot behind Eddie's, however, while his powers of recovery were considerable.'

In 1939, in Milan, Male was involved in an incident that echoed down the years. Playing against Italy, he moved to cover the big centre-forward Silvio Piola as Michele Andreolo, Italy's Uruguayan born centre-half, sent a long pass down the middle. As Piola moved to the ball in turn, he slipped, stuck out his arm and punched the ball over his shoulder into the net, following through to hit Male in the eye. Dr Pecos Bauwens, the German referee, gave a goal that so enraged the Italian Crown Prince that it took Stanley Rous, the Football Association's secretary, to restrain him from running on to the field to protest. Male received a black eye but was always, typically, at pains to emphasise that Piola had not meant it. Piola, for his part, joked about it years later.

Male gained consolation for the disappointments of the 1932 Cup final when he played an outstanding game for Arsenal in the final of 1936 at Wembley, when Sheffield United were beaten, with great difficulty, 1-0. He also won Championship medals in Arsenal's hat-trick of victories between 1933 and 1935, missing only 10 league games in those three seasons. Altogether he played 285 First Division matches, scoring 19 goals.

On retirement he looked after the third team, training on the Golders Green (later Hendon) ground at Claremont Road, Cricklewood, an ever benign and tolerant presence. When he finally left the club he emigrated to Canada to live with his son.

George Male, born May 8 1910, died February 19 1998

Knowing his woodwork

GEORGE MARKS

George Marks, who has died aged 82, might be described as England's great forgotten goalkeeper. While his successor Frank Swift, who died in the Munich air crash, is remembered and venerated, Marks's eight international appearances are little recalled.

Born at Figheldean near Salisbury, Marks was originally a carpenter. At just under 6ft he was no giant for a goalkeeper and in his prime weighed 12st 10lb. He played amateur football for Salisbury Corinthians until Arsenal spotted him and, in the last pre-war football season, gave him two appearances in their First Division team. When the war began, Marks displaced George Swindin as the team's first-choice goalkeeper.

Marks was never flamboyant, never a 'character'. He simply did his job, a powerfully built and agile figure, dark hair creamed neatly back in the fashion of the time, brave in the box, dominant in the air, possessed of a powerful goal-kick. Then, like many Arsenal players, he joined the Royal Air Force, for whose strong representative team he often played.

Despite appearing several times in England teams, he never won a full international cap as they were not awarded during the war. He appeared in all England's international games in 1941-42, in the last of which, in Cardiff, he was injured. Wales won 1-0 and beat England again the next autumn 2-1 at Wolverhampton. He went back to Wembley at the end of the season to play for the Arsenal team that won the League South Cup final, crushing Charlton Athletic 7-1. He was also the regular goalkeeper in Arsenal's League South winning side.

Later in the war he, like Swindin, was sent abroad. When the FA Cup was revived in January 1946, both goalkeepers were still in Europe. Arsenal, drawn against West Ham United, decided that whichever goalkeeper got back to London first should fill the part. In the event it was Swindin, who let through half a dozen goals as Arsenal lost 6-0.

Tom Whittaker, the club's legendary trainer and later manager, said Swindin would play in the return match, just as a pilot who crashed should immediately be sent up in another aeroplane. This time Arsenal won 1-0, Swindin kept his place for seasons to come and Arsenal sold Marks to Blackburn Rovers, where his old England and Arsenal captain, Eddie Hapgood, had just become manager. Both may have had bittersweet feelings when, in the second match of the 1946-47 league campaign, Arsenal lost 3-1 to Blackburn, Marks playing solidly in goal.

In 1948 Marks moved to Bristol City but, within months, he had been transferred again, this time to Reading, of the Third Division South, where he became a popular and respected figure.

'You could forget about George Marks,' Reading's trainer once said, meaning you could always rely on him. But in another sense Marks has been unkindly forgotten. Had it not been for an injured eye, and the war, much more would surely have been heard of him.

George Marks, born April 9 1915, died January 31 1998

Physio who doubled up

BERTIE MEE

How much does a football manager do? It is a question that recurs and was asked conspicuously when Arsenal, in the 1970-71 season, won the FA Cup and League Championship Double 10 years after their north London rivals, Tottenham Hotspur, had achieved it. The Gunners' manager was Bertie Mee, who has died aged 82. Arsenal, who had not won a domestic trophy since 1953, beat their rivals 1-0 to clinch the title and five days later defeated Liverpool at Wembley to lift the FA Cup.

Mee had succeeded Billy Wright five years earlier, in June 1966. The contrast could not have been greater. Mee had never been more than a peripheral player, an outside-right of sorts with Derby County. Wright, by contrast, had won 105 caps, captaining England with panache and figuring in three World Cups. But where Wright during his four years at Highbury, his first managerial position, had seemed a tyro struggling to assert himself, Mee, stepping up from club physiotherapist, proved a formidable organiser from the start even if he would never make the public impact of such formidable predecessors as Herbert Chapman or win the affection of such as Tom Whittaker, in charge of the team in the late 1940s.

Here an analogy is relevant. Whittaker, from the north-east, had been a moderate left-half whom Chapman, after Whittaker had broken a leg on tour with an FA team in Australia, persuaded to become the outstanding trainer of his times, a man with 'magic hands' who, in an era when technology was still in its infancy, could bring injured players back to fitness in record time. Mee himself was a physiotherapist, and an outstanding one, though he had the advantage of sophisticated technology. Whittaker, beloved by his players, became manager and promptly won the Championship whereas Mee, a steely character and far less of a father figure, was destined not only to win that double but to survive in his role as manager for a decade.

He was born in Bulwell, Nottinghamshire. His career as a footballer with Derby County was cut short by an injury and after six years serving with the Royal Army Medical Corps he qualified as a physiotherapist. Mee joined Arsenal as a trainer in 1960 before becoming the team's physiotherapist and then manager. In his first season he brought in key players: George Graham, Colin Addison and Bob McNab. Later he 'brought on' Charlie George and, under the captaincy of Frank McLintock, developed an effective partnership between Ray Kennedy and John Radford, converting the former full-back Peter Storey into a midfield anchorman.

As a manager Mee was often praised for his man management but seldom for his knowledge of the game or tactical flair. When Arsenal won the Double, it was thanks to a productive partnership with his coach Don Howe, the former England right-back, in charge of youth football at Highbury.

In the famous 1970-71 season Arsenal were perhaps unfairly criticised for their 'cautious' tactics. In fact, in George, Eddie Kelly, Graham and the winger George Armstrong they had particularly creative players.

At Highbury Mee kept the heat off Howe: it is all too easy to underestimate this function in a manager who, in the last analysis, must take the brickbats as well as the plaudits. But at the FA Cup final banquet in 1971, after the Gunners had beaten Liverpool, Howe was mortified when the club chairman, Denis Hill-Wood, made no mention of him in his speech. That was the end for Howe, who left to manage his old club West Bromwich Albion. When apprised of Howe's departure, Mee brushed it aside but, although he would survive at Highbury for another five years, things would never be the same again.

When things went wrong Mee could be peppery with the press: 'I know you're only doing your job, I know you have to make a living.' Charm was never his forte but as an administrator he was formidable. Moreover his players long admired him for his pugnacious courage after an appalling episode in Rome in 1970, when Arsenal had drawn 2-2 with Lazio in a torrid European Cup match. At the end of the official banquet the Lazio players attacked the Arsenal team and a bitter battle broke out outside the restaurant. Mee, fists flailing, played a gallant part in it.

Arsenal, who had won the Inter-Cities Fairs Cup the previous season – reversing a 3-1 defeat by Anderlecht in Brussels in the first leg of the final with a 3-0 win at Highbury – proceeded to beat Lazio 2-0 in the return leg before eventually going out to FC Köln on away goals in the quarter-finals.

Unsurprisingly Arsenal's Double season earned Mee the title of football manager of the year. It was the only year he would win the award, although he twice took the team to the Football League Cup final and saw them finish runners-up in the league in 1973. By the time he resigned from Arsenal in 1976, however, the team had sunk to 17th place. In 1986 Mee became the general manager of Watford and remained a director there until 1991. He is survived by his wife, Doris, and two daughters, Alison and Beverley.

Bertie Mee, born December 25 1918, died October 21 2001

APRIL 2 2001

Rocky romance

DAVID ROCASTLE

David 'Rocky' Rocastle, who has died from non-Hodgkin's lymphoma aged 33, perhaps never quite came to terms with his ejection from Arsenal. That he is well remembered and admired at Highbury was shown when the 38,000 crowd there, before the north London derby with Tottenham Hotspur, observed a minute's silence without the faintest interruption. David Pleat, manager of Tottenham for the day, had suggested to the referee, Paul Durkin, before the match that he blow his whistle as soon as there was any interruption to the silence, believing that football crowds, in such circumstances, could seldom observe more than half a minute. Pleat had underestimated them.

Born in Lewisham, south-east London, Rocastle, a fast, skilled, powerful outside-right who won 14 caps for England, was one of three black players from the same area who played a crucial part in Arsenal's success in the late 1980s and early 1990s. Rocastle, the clever playmaker Paul Davis and the powerful midfielder Michael Thomas represented a new and positive trend at Highbury, following on the Irish 'tendency', as represented by David O'Leary, Frank Stapleton and Liam Brady.

Rocastle joined Arsenal as an apprentice in August 1983, turned professional with them on December 31 1984 and remained at Highbury until, deeply against his wishes, he was transferred to Leeds United in July 1992. He played a leading role in Arsenal's winning of the League Championship in 1988-89, not least in their extraordinary decisive victory over Liverpool at

Anfield in the final match of the league season. It was one which they had to win by two goals to take the title and this they did with a goal at the last gasp by Thomas. A famous photograph shows Thomas and Rocastle celebrating at the final whistle. In that Championship season Rocastle played 38 games, scoring half a dozen goals. In 1990-91, when Arsenal won the Championship again, he played 13 full games, made three appearances as substitute and scored a couple of goals.

One great disappointment was that he missed playing for England in the 1990 World Cup in Italy. He was one of 26 players chosen by the manager, Bobby Robson, to go to training camp before the tournament but was then one of four dropped when the squad was reduced to 22.

Altogether Rocastle made 204 appearances for Arsenal in the League, plus 14 as substitute, scoring 24 goals. He helped them to win the Football League Cup in 1987 and was in the team beaten in the 1988 final. His overall total of games in all tournaments for Arsenal was 260, with 17 appearances as substitute, scoring 34 goals. Despite a strong, right-footed shot he specialised more in making opportunities from the wing for other players. It would be wrong to call him, generically, a midfielder. He was very much in the tradition of Arsenal outside-rights, from Joe Hulme and Alf Kirchen onwards.

When Rocastle was transferred to Leeds, Davis recalled, 'he cried. We spoke about it quite often. He couldn't understand why they ever wanted him to go. The club's line was that he was injured, he was struggling with his weight and he'd had a knee operation. In his own mind I don't think he ever recovered from the fact of leaving Arsenal. He was a bubbly character, lovely spirit, fantastic spirit and really he was an Arsenal person. I always remember when he left the club: it was one of the saddest moments for him.'

From Leeds Rocastle went on to play for Manchester City, in December 1993, moving back to London – but to Chelsea – in August 1994, where it gradually grew plain that something of the spark had gone. In January 1997 he went, for a spell, to Norwich City, signed for Hull City in October 1997 and finished his playing career in Malaysia.

On or off the field it was hard to upset him. He was pleasant, modest and humorous. Alan Hansen relates that when, playing against him for Liverpool, he brought him down quite badly, Rocastle merely smiled at him and asked: 'Getting old?'

He leaves a wife, Janet, and three children.

David Rocastle, born May 2 1967, died March 31 2001

JUNE 27 2001

Don Roper

HUNGRY WINGER

Don Roper, who has died aged 78 after suffering from Parkinson's disease, played a crucial role in Arsenal's successes in the immediate post-war years. A two-footed winger, who made his name on the right but latterly played for the Gunners at outside-left, he was noted for the power of his shot and the accuracy of his crosses. There was, for example, a spectacular goal he scored against Derby County – a ferocious left-footed shot from more than 30 yards which tore past the Derby goalkeeper Jock Wallace to finish in the top corner.

A Hampshire man, born in Botley, Roper was initially a centre-forward and was discovered playing for Bitterne Nomads in the Hampshire League by scouts for Southampton. He turned professional with the Saints in 1940, at the age of 17, making several first-team appearances in wartime football at centre-forward. In 1943, however, the club switched him to the right wing, where he immediately flourished, establishing a fruitful partnership with the inside-right Ted Bates, who eventually became Southampton's manager.

Arsenal pursued Roper for several years until, in the summer of 1947, their new manager and former trainer Tom Whittaker signed him after what was described as 'one of the most drawn-out and delicate deals in the history of football transfers'. The sticking point seemed to concern which Arsenal player would go to Southampton in part exchange; eventually the lot fell on the skilful young inside-forward George Curtis, who spent many successful years at The Dell.

Arsenal had begun the previous season disastrously and at one time looked in danger of relegation, a fate which had not befallen them since their controversial induction, then promotion, to the First Division in 1919. Now Roper and another significant transfer, the Scottish international right-half Archie Macaulay, galvanised a team that went on to win that season's Championship. Roper made 40 appearances and scored 10 goals.

A quiet and modest man, he was renowned at Highbury for his gargantuan appetite. The story was told that, when Arsenal players were entertained to Christmas dinner by the club captain, Joe Mercer, and his wife, she brought out a plate heaped almost to overflowing. 'Crikey,' said Roper, 'the bloke that eats that must be an absolute glutton.' 'Well actually, Don,' said Barbara Mercer, 'it's yours.'

Roper lost his place to Freddie Cox in the Arsenal team that won the 1950 Cup final but two years later he was back in the team which, reduced to 10 men for much of the match, lost 1-0 to Newcastle United at Wembley. When moved to right-back in place of the injured Walley Barnes, Roper had an outstanding game. Switched to the left-back position against Blackpool in October

1949, he successfully nullified Stanley Matthews and made the winning goal from a corner.

In October 1952, at Highbury, in a friendly game against Hibernian – and one of the first to be televised in the evening – Roper scored five times against the reigning Scotland goalkeeper, Tommy Younger. That season also saw him win a second Championship medal, scoring 14 goals in 41 appearances, and play for England B against Scotland B in March 1953.

Though a strong and essentially straightforward winger, his technique was not to be despised and, on one occasion at White Hart Lane, he ran rings round Alf Ramsey, then the England right-back. In his 10 years at Highbury Roper scored 88 goals in 297 league appearances.

In 1956 he went back for a couple of seasons to Southampton, coached minor teams for a short while, then went into a local engineering firm that sadly collapsed in the 1980s, forcing him into early retirement. He is survived by his widow, Joyce, and two sons, Donald and Leslie.

Don Roper, born December 14 1922, died June 8 2001

OCTOBER 31 2005

Card-index mind on angles

GEORGE SWINDIN

George Swindin, who has died aged 90, was Arsenal's brave, resilient goalkeeper in the immediate post-war years and became their manager in 1958. He won his first League Championship medal as far back as 1938, to which he added a second 10 years later, and he made 14 appearances when Arsenal won the Championship again in 1953, by which time his first-team place had gone to the young Welsh international, Jack Kelsey. Swindin also won an FA Cup medal in 1950, when Arsenal beat Liverpool 2-0, and a runners-up medal two years later when, down to 10 men for most of the game, they were beaten 1-0 by Newcastle United.

He was born in Campsall, near Doncaster, and began his playing career with Rotherham YMCA, New Stubbin Colliery and, still as an amateur, with Rotherham United. Swindin came to the attention of the major clubs as goalkeeper for Bradford City from 1934 and, after he had played 26 league games for them, Arsenal signed him in April 1936. The following season he made his First Division debut at Brentford. The one after saw him making 17 appearances, sharing the goalkeeping with Frank Boulton and Alex Wilson, enough for a Championship medal. In the last pre-war season he made 21 league appearances, with Wilson playing 19 games and George Marks, Arsenal's and England's first-choice goalkeeper in the first years of the war, only two.

At the end of the war Marks, in the RAF, seemed to be favoured over Swindin, an army PT instructor. It was a question of who got back to London first for the third-round FA Cup tie at West Ham. Swindin did, only to let in six without reply. Had it not been for Swindin, the margin might have been greater. Tom Whittaker, the Arsenal trainer who would, in 1947, become manager, was an RAF officer. 'When a pilot crashes, you don't keep him on the ground for a time; you send him up again at once so that he regains his confidence. That's what we are doing with George Swindin.'

Not that Swindin had lost his confidence, which was always high. He had a resilient game at Tottenham and stayed in the Arsenal goal while Marks was transferred to Blackburn Rovers for £5,000, then a record fee for a goalkeeper.

When league football restarted the following season, Arsenal had every reason to be grateful for Swindin's brave and expert keeping.

Having missed only four league matches in 1946-47, he played all 42 the following season as, under Whittaker, a revitalised Arsenal strode to the championship. It was a tribute to Swindin's condition and powers of recovery. His courage was enormous, his speciality the blocking of a shot at full pelt, which obviated the need to make a save on the line. One of his team-mates said: 'George has a card-index mind on angles. He is quick to make up his mind and, as soon as he has, he acts. Ninety-nine times out of a hundred he is right.'

Perhaps the finest and most spectacular save he ever made was during that season from Tommy Lawton at Chelsea, where he hurtled through the air to deflect a seemingly irresistible header for a corner, via the outside of a post. The only blemish came in the sixth league game and the sixth Arsenal win. Rushing out to gather the ball, he collided with the stand-in Arsenal centre-half, Alf Fields, who was covering for Leslie Compton. Fields' knee was badly injured and he did not play again that season.

Kicks on the hands, kicks on the body, kicks even on the head Swindin seemed to shrug off almost casually. He had an especially memorable game in 1949 in Sao Paulo against the Corinthians, on Arsenal's tour of Brazil. At the end of it the rest of the team lined up to pat him on the back. The game was watched by 80,000 people.

By the time he left Arsenal in February 1954 to become player-manager of Peterborough United, Swindin had played 272 league games for the Gunners. In 1958 he returned to Highbury as manager, a role in which he was somewhat less successful.

Leaving Arsenal in April 1962, he became manager of Second Division Norwich City that May but, after 20 games, he took over as manager of Cardiff City. At Cardiff he signed John Charles from Roma but Swindin's appointment ended, with some bitterness, in 1964. He went on to manage Kettering and Corby, as well as a Corby garage, before retiring to Spain.

He is survived by his wife, Stella, and his son.

George Swindin, born December 4 1914, died October 26 2005

3

Pride of Scotland

A famous fifth

BOBBY JOHNSTONE

Though Bobby Johnstone, who has died aged 71, won 17 Scotland caps and scored in successive mid-1950s FA Cup finals for Manchester City, his place in footballing legend is assured by his membership of the 'famous five', the Hibernian forward line that made its collective debut in a 2-0 win over Queen of the South on October 15 1949.

Johnstone had all the qualities of the classical Scottish inside-forward – elegant ball control, supreme balance and the ability to score goals – that earned him a place between Gordon Smith on the right wing and the quick little centre-forward Lawrie Reilly, with Eddie Turnbull (who would go on to an Indian summer at right-half) at inside-left and Willie Ormond, a future Scotland manager, on the left wing.

Born and brought up in Selkirk, Johnstone played non-league football for the town (which he also represented as a fine cricketer) while serving his apprenticeship as a painter. He signed professional terms for Hibernian in 1946 and his precocious skills were evident as a teenager when playing for a post-war British Army side at Tottenham during his national service. This lasted from 1947-49. Though he was first sent to Yeovil, a posting to Edinburgh Castle enabled him to maintain the Hibs connection.

His first-team debut came against Partick Thistle in 1949. Once the 'famous five' were lined up, the Edinburgh club came within a point of winning the Scottish League in 1949-50 and took the title in 1951 and 1952 before, in 1953, being pipped by Rangers on goal average.

Johnstone's first cap came in April on a memorable day for Scottish football, when both he and Reilly scored in a 3-2 win at Wembley over England, who were notably lacking Wilf Mannion, Johnstone's virtual equivalent as a player. Two more appearances followed on Scotland's European tour and of the 17 he made in total 14 came while he was with Hibernian. Sadly he did not go to Switzerland with the World Cup team in 1954; had he done so, the Scots might not have suffered so badly.

In March 1955 he was transferred from Hibernian to Manchester City for £22,000. Within weeks he scored his team's goal in response to three by Newcastle United in the Cup final. A winner's medal came the following year when his two goals, one a spectacular header, contributed to a reversed scoreline of 3-1 in City's famous 'Revie plan' win over Birmingham City. This made him the first player to score in successive FA Cup finals.

When Revie was missing, Johnstone was perfectly capable of taking his place as deep-lying, creative centre-forward. He could operate successfully on the right wing, too. While with City he played 124 league games, scoring 42 goals, and gained his last three Scottish caps, all in the 1956 home international tournament.

A second spell with Hibernian lasted just over a season, from September 1959, though it did enable Johnstone to take his tally of league goals for the club to 100. In all competitions he finished with 132. His final professional home was at Oldham Athletic, whom he joined in October 1960. He brought flair to the team, making goals with penetrating passes and scoring 36 of his own in 143 league games. In 1963 Oldham won promotion to the Third Division. In May 1965 Johnstone left league football.

Injury prevented him from continuing semi-professionally for Witton Albion but he remained in Lancashire as a fish wholesaler before returning to Selkirk last year. His marriage to his wife, Heather, ended in divorce in 1985. His daughter, Nicola, survives him.

Robert 'Bobby' Johnstone, born September 7 1929, died August
22 2001

MARCH 14 2006

Jinky, lord of the wing

JIMMY JOHNSTONE

The little, red-haired Scotsman Jimmy Johnstone, who has died aged
61, was an integral member of the remarkable Celtic team that won
nine Scottish Championships in a row between 1966 and 1974. He
was also one of the Lisbon Lions, the Celtic team that became the
first British side to lift the European Cup in 1967. A classical winger,
famed for his dynamic speed, immaculate control and ability to go
outside the opposing full-back, he was capped 23 times for Scotland
and scored 129 goals in 515 appearances for Celtic. In a poll among
the fans in 2002 he was voted the club's best ever player.

Off the field Johnstone was never the most docile of players,
clashing time and again with Celtic's illustrious manager Jock
Stein – to the point that Stein's own mother once rebuked him: 'I
think you're very hard on that wee fellow.' Stein, who knew how
effective Johnstone could be, 'especially against continentals',
once dropped him because 'he was doing things he wasn't
supposed to do'. And there was a comical occasion when, in training camp with the Scotland team at Largs a month before the
World Cup finals in West Germany in 1974, Johnstone went out
in a boat, found himself adrift and had to be rescued.

He was born in Uddingston, near Glasgow, and was signed as a
teenager, at 5ft 4in and weighing 9st 7lb, by Celtic in 1961 after

Manchester United had expressed an interest. Johnstone made his debut in the 1962-63 season, playing four games for one goal. The following season saw him fully established in the side, playing 25 for half a dozen goals – and so it went on for many seasons. Winning Scotland under-23 caps in that first full season, he made his debut for the full national side against Wales in October 1964, displacing the usual incumbent, another clever right-winger, Rangers' Willie Henderson.

Johnstone made only sporadic appearances for Scotland, even though his solitary game in the 1965-66 season (against England at Hampden Park) saw him score two spectacular goals and, at least in the second half, confirm the dominance over the hapless England left-back, Keith Newton, that he had shown a few weeks earlier at Newcastle, when the Scottish League beat the Football League 3-1.

Oddly Johnstone's performance at Hampden Park that day took some time to ignite. Early in the second half he missed a good heading chance, enabling England to break away and score. But, when Denis Law slipped him through a square England defence, Johnstone at last showed his pace and power, racing away to beat Gordon Banks from close range. With Scotland 4-2 down and time running out, Johnstone scored again, the reward for his persistence. Jim Baxter's free-kick floated over a static English defence, enabling Johnstone to chase it, catch the ball almost on the goal-line and smash it home off the underside of the bar.

The following season saw Celtic's triumphant path to the European Cup final. In Nantes, in the first leg of the second round, Johnstone's form was irresistible and earned him the nickname of the Flying Flea with the French. In the Lisbon final against Inter Milan Johnstone and the other Celtic winger, Bobby Lennox, had orders to move into the middle, leaving the flanks to the attacking full-backs. Celtic deservedly won 2-1. They then contested the ill-starred Intercontinental Cup a few months later. The notorious play-off against Racing Club of Buenos Aires in Montevideo saw Johnstone forced to wash the spittle out of his hair at half-time and sent off in the second half.

Celtic reached the European Cup final again in 1970, losing 2-1 after extra-time to the Dutch team Feyenoord. The campaign was notable for their double victory against the then dominant Leeds United in the semi-finals. Johnstone was outstanding in both games. In the first leg at Elland Road he tirelessly used the whole of the right touchline, often dropping deep to collect the ball, tormenting Leeds' England left-back Terry Cooper, who did not dare to overlap in his usual manner. At Hampden Park in the return Johnstone was just as effective.

Brian Wilson, a Scottish football writer, recalls Johnstone's own take on his career and how his talent had been honed in an era when there was not a lot of money about. 'Football was the greatest part of our lives, just like the boys from Brazil and Spain,' Johnstone had said. 'They lived in poverty, like us, and that's where all the great players came from – the street.'

The Lisbon Lions not only all came from Glasgow and its environs but remained a close-knit unit throughout their lives, probably because they were all from essentially the same background. 'I look back now,' said Johnstone, 'and think, "Bloody hell, we did achieve great things." But at the time we were just an ordinary bunch of lads.'

Jinky, as he was affectionately known, was given a free transfer at the end of the 1974-75 season and then played for San Jose Earthquakes, Sheffield United, Dundee, Shelbourne and Elgin City. He was diagnosed in November 2001 with motor neurone disease, which gradually confined him to his home in Lanarkshire. Some consolation came in the 90-minute documentary film of his playing career, Lord of the Wing, in 2004, in which he was praised by such stars as Alfredo di Stéfano, Eusebio and Law. His infectious personality and sense of humour made him a huge and continuing favourite. He is survived by his wife, Agnes, a son and two daughters.

James Connolly Johnstone, born September 30 1944, died March 12 2006

5 July 2001

Liverpool raider

Billy Liddell

Billy Liddell, who has died aged 79 after suffering from Alzheimer's disease, was so esteemed at Liverpool that the team was nicknamed 'Liddellpool'. He was almost too good to be true, the perfect sportsman – fast, hard but impeccably fair – a convinced Christian, a diligent worker with boys' clubs, a wartime Bomber Command pilot officer and pathfinder, and a teetotaller who, when he beat Liverpool's appearance record held by the goalkeeper Elisha Scott, was presented, *inter alia*, with a cocktail cabinet.

Liddell was a winger in the old 'raiding' tradition of pace, power and incisiveness, a left-winger of choice who could play just as well on the right and eventually became a successful centre-forward.

He was born at Townhill, near Dunfermline, the eldest of six children of a coal miner who eventually died of silicosis and was determined Billy would not go down the pits. Billy's first club was Kingseat Juniors, who paid him half a crown (12.5p) per game. As a 15-year-old he was spotted playing for the Lochgelly Violet club, by Matt Busby, destined to become the famous manager of Manchester United but then a half-back with Liverpool. Busby had been due to play golf with a former team-mate at Manchester City,

Alex Herd, but Herd did not appear. Instead Busby went with the manager of Hamilton Academical, Willie McAndrew, to look at the young Liddell. Hamilton could not offer Billy the part-time job on which his father insisted, so Busby recommended him to Liverpool and there he stayed for the whole of his career, although he did play as a guest for Chelsea during the Second World War.

Liddell first played for Scotland in April 1942, an unofficial cap at Hampden Park in one of Scotland's rare wartime victories against England: 5-4 and Liddell got one of the goals.

The war over and with football resuming on a full basis in 1946, Liddell settled down on Liverpool's left wing, a torment to any full-back and a special nightmare for Alf Ramsey when Tottenham's and England's right-back. 'I always knew I was in for a hectic after-noon when I was marking Billy,' Ramsey said. 'The only way to try to hold him was to beat him to possession of the ball. Once he had it, he was difficult to stop.'

Liverpool that season won a Championship protracted into summer by appalling weather. Liddell played 34 games for seven goals but by the time he finished playing for the team in 1960 he had scored 216 in 495 games. The cry from the Kop, 'Give it to Billy', had become endearingly familiar.

In May 1947 Liddell was on the left wing for Great Britain against the Rest of Europe, contributing to a 6-1 victory. Remarkably he was picked for Britain again, in 1955 in Belfast, though on that occasion the Europeans won 4-1.

Things might have gone differently in the 1950 FA Cup final at Wembley had Liddell not been painfully fouled by the Arsenal right-half, a fellow Scotsman, Alex Forbes. 'I couldn't put my jacket on the next day,' he later recalled. 'Lucky Arsenal?' wrote JPW Mallalieu in *The Spectator*. 'No, just a little dirty.' Liverpool lost 2-0. By contrast, when Liddell broke the ribs of the England goalkeeper Frank Swift in a collision in an international at Hampden, Swift was quick to say: 'It was fair. Billy doesn't know how to be anything but fair.'

In 1958 Liddell was appointed a justice of the peace. He had successfully combined his football career with working as an accountant and it was as such, when he finished playing, that he operated as a bursar at Liverpool University, watching Liverpool as a modest season ticket holder.

For Scotland he played 28 games, scoring half a dozen goals, but he never appeared in a World Cup. Standing 5ft 10in and weighing 12st 9lb, Liddell in full flight drove through defences like a preoccupied tank. 'There was no weakness in Billy's game,' said Busby. 'He was as strong as a bull on the ball. Defenders found him a real handful but always respected him.' Billy Wright, captain of England and often an opponent of Liddell, said: 'Scotland have had few greater players. He could conjure goals out of nothing' – not only with both feet but with his head. He once headed a goal from outside the penalty box.

Liddell leaves a wife and twin sons.

Billy Liddell, born January 10 1922, died July 3 2001

FEBRUARY 3 2004

Ayr's and crashes

ALLY MACLEOD

Ally MacLeod, who has died aged 72, was a talented outside-left, a star of the 1960 FA Cup final for beaten Blackburn Rovers and manager of a string of Scottish clubs but it was his misfortune to be remembered above all for the anticlimax of the 1978 World

Cup finals in Argentina, when Scotland, of whom he was manager, went out in the first round. This came after sustained euphoria, much of it generated by MacLeod himself.

It might be argued that, for all their previous successes under MacLeod, Scotland were lucky even to go to the World Cup. Their victory in a decisive qualifying game against Wales was facilitated by a notorious penalty awarded by the French referee even though the offending upstretched hand that had touched the ball was that of the Scottish centre-forward Joe Jordan, not a Welsh defender.

MacLeod talked in grandiose manner of defending the World Cup after his team had won it, though the loss of the outstanding Celtic right-back Danny McGrain, through injury, was compounded by MacLeod's decision not to take the powerful centre-forward Andy Gray. 'I'm a winner,' MacLeod proclaimed.

He certainly made a lot of money, buying a public house for an estimated £70,000, though he insisted it was rented and the cost exaggerated. Around the Scottish camp hung such an aura of materialism, of wheeling and dealing, that it was strange to read a subsequent report by the Scottish FA, blaming MacLeod for not making clear to his players how much they stood to earn.

Over-confidence and erratic team selection had much to do with Scotland's initial defeat against Peru, in Cordoba. Inexplicably MacLeod chose in midfield Don Masson and Bruce Rioch, both in such poor previous form that Derby County had put them on the transfer list. Yet they were preferred to Graeme Souness, a major figure in Liverpool's conquest of the European Cup. In particular Teofilo Cubillas, the gifted Peruvian who had been a star of the 1970 World Cup, was plainly underestimated for he ran Scotland ragged. And Martin Buchan, a centre-half played out of position at left-back, complained he had not known the right-winger Juan José Muñante was so fast.

The Scots, starting well and going ahead with a goal by Jordan, fell away, missed a penalty through Masson and succumbed to two goals by Cubillas. They looked even worse against Iran, struggling to a 1-1 draw, but rose too late to beat the powerful Dutch 3-2 with a superlative goal by little Archie Gemmill.

Born in Glasgow, MacLeod joined his nearby club Third Lanark as a schoolboy, did his military service with the Royal Scots, signed for St Mirren and went thence to Blackburn Rovers. In dispute with them over a pay offer, he moved back to Hibernian, Third Lanark again and Ayr United, who appointed him manager in 1967. There he stayed for nine productive years, becoming Ayr's 1973 Citizen of the Year, before transferring in 1976 to Aberdeen, winning the League Cup and finishing runners-up in the Championship. Later he managed Motherwell, Airdrie, Ayr again and Queen of the South. He had latterly been suffering from Alzheimer's disease. He is survived by his wife, Faye, two sons and a daughter.

Alistair Reid MacLeod, born February 26 1931, died February 1 2004

MAY 17 2001

Drive and vision

BOBBY MURDOCH

Bobby Murdoch, who has died in hospital at 56 after a stroke, was one of the crucial elements in the fine Celtic team which, in May 1967, became the first British club to win the European Cup, beating Internazionale of Milan 2-1 in Lisbon. Their nickname, the Lions of Lisbon, has survived the years, as indeed have the admiration and affection in which Murdoch was held by other members of that Celtic team. Inter were strong favourites and took the lead. In the second half Tommy Gemmell put the sides level and the winning goal came when Murdoch, who was exerting growing authority, shot and Steve Chalmers diverted the ball home. Jock Stein, Celtic's manager and architect of their success, described Murdoch that evening as the team's best player.

It was Stein who successfully converted Murdoch from an inside-right into a right-half, controlling the midfield play with his excellent technique and perceptive passing. Bobby Lennox, the outside-left of that team, has said: 'To watch Bobby was an education. He could shape to make a pass with his right foot and then turn on a sixpence and make the same pass with his left. He had radar vision, marvellous at putting long balls into a clear space. He helped me a lot.' As indeed he did his whole team.

Murdoch was born in Rutherglen and began playing for his school under-12s at seven. He left school at 15 and took a job as a sheet metalworker. At about the same time he began training with Motherwell but soon signed for Celtic, turning professional at 17. He made his debut in 1961. The following year Murdoch badly damaged his right ankle in a collision with the Hearts goalkeeper, Gordon Marshall. The injury never really mended but he played on. In 1995 a tribunal decided that this was an industrial injury, which entitled him to compensation. 'I had to play through the pain barrier,' he said. 'This is a victory for all injured footballers.'

It was surprising that he should win only a dozen caps for Scotland, the first in 1965 against Wales, the last in the 1969-70 season versus Austria. In April 1969 his powerfully struck goal gave Scotland a 1-1 draw against West Germany in a World Cup eliminator in Glasgow.

The Scottish reporter Brian Wilson described him as 'the dynamo of a team which came, almost exclusively, from within a 30-mile radius of Glasgow. Celtic had a youth policy that bequeathed Stein a pool of gifted players, including Murdoch, all of them devoted to Celtic. Stein's genius lay in identifying their strengths and drawing out their full potential. Murdoch's strength was in the way he could pass a ball, splitting defences with devastating precision. He filled the gap left by Pat Crerand, whose loss to Manchester United had been sorely felt by the Celtic support. Murdoch was more than equal to the challenge.'

He made 484 appearances for Celtic between 1962 and 1973, scoring 105 goals. He won eight Championships, four Scottish Cups, five League Cups and was Scotland's player of the year in 1969.

In September 1973, to his dismay, Stein gave him a free transfer to Middlesbrough. 'I think Jock wanted more runners in the team,' he said, 'but that didn't really make sense to me, because you can cover the ground a lot faster with a good pass than you can by running.'

He was Jack Charlton's first signing, scored on his home debut and missed only two games that season, when Middlesbrough won the Second Division title. He finished his playing career in 1975, after almost 100 games for Middlesbrough, then joined their coaching staff. In 1981 he became manager but in his first season in charge the side were relegated. The following season he was just about to tee off on a golf course when he was called back to the club and dismissed.

His health was often poor: hip trouble forced him for a time after retirement to walk with a stick, he had to conquer alcohol problems and by the summer of 1987 his life was a disaster. The pub he ran had failed, he had been made bankrupt and his wife Kathleen had left him, though his son John stayed by his side. In the past, beset by weight troubles, he had frequently gone to a health farm in Hertfordshire. He is survived by Kathleen, two sons and a daughter.

Robert White Murdoch, born August 17 1944, died May 15 2001

SEPTEMBER 18 2001

Wide Ranger

ALEX SCOTT

Alex Scott, who has died of cancer aged 64, was the Glasgow Rangers and Scotland outside-right who came between Willie Waddell and Willie Henderson – all internationals of distinction, though the well-built Scott, 5ft 9in and 12st, was closer in style to the powerful Waddell than to the electrically elusive little Henderson.

Born in Falkirk and educated at Bainsford primary and Falkirk technical schools, in the early 1950s he made his debut against his home-town club, with Rangers, scoring three goals in a 4-1 win. He was capped for Scotland while playing, as a teenager, for Rangers' reserves. Altogether he played 331 games for Rangers, winning four Championship medals.

Scott's international career began against Northern Ireland in 1956, a season in which he won two more caps. In 1957 he was capped twice more but did not take part in the 1958 World Cup finals in Sweden. The next season saw him make a single appearance for his country, against Portugal, then two seasons passed before, in 1961-62, he was capped five times and made his only appearance against England, at Hampden Park.

The emergence of Henderson led to Scott's transfer to Everton early enough in 1963 to help Everton win the League Championship, making 17 appearances, scoring four goals and deploying his pace and ability to pick out a colleague. The following season he even regained his position in the Scotland team, eventually taking his total caps to 16, and in the spring of 1966 he was in the Everton side that won a see-saw Cup final 3-2 against Sheffield Wednesday.

On that occasion Scott may well have had an impression of *déjà vu*, since he spent most of the game stationed wide on the right. Back in 1959-60, when Rangers reached the European Cup semi-final – losing to Eintracht Frankfurt – the Rangers left-half Willie Stevenson recalled: 'When you look back at that year, our lack of knowledge was laughable. Alex Scott, for instance, had tremendous ability to beat a man but he was not allowed to stray from his touchline and intrude on other people's territory.'

In general, though, with Everton Scott proved quite capable of intruding if he felt a team-mate was playing selfishly. In a game against Tottenham in January 1965 he became so exasperated by the individualism of his big centre-forward Fred Pickering that he simply tackled his own man. The stratagem seemed to work as from that point the two combined sweetly and Scott gave Cyril Knowles, Spurs' English international left-back, a torrid afternoon.

After Everton Scott played for Hibernian and Falkirk. In retirement he ran a pub in his home town with his brother James, another former professional player. His wife, Annette, survives him, as do his twin sons and three granddaughters.

Alex Scott, born November 22 1936, died September 12 2001

MARCH 24 1998

Cardiff's Scottish survivor

JIMMY SCOULAR

Jimmy Scoular, who has died aged 73, will be chiefly remembered as the classical type of Scottish wing-half – powerful and relentless in the tackle, economical rather than inspired in his steady use of the ball. In the days of the third-back game and W formation, it was the inside-forward, rather than the wing-half, who was expected to be inventive.

Born in Livingston, Scoular joined the Royal Navy during the last war. Portsmouth managers, who spotted him playing in local, naval games in Hampshire, persuaded him to join them as a professional in 1945. He proved a more than competent successor to another Scottish right-half, Jimmy Guthrie, who had captained Pompey to their surprising 4-1 win against Wolves at Wembley in the 1939 FA Cup final.

Scoular became a dynamic figure in a famous half-back line consisting of himself, Reg Flewin at centre-half and Jimmy Dickinson at left-half. He and Dickinson complemented each other perfectly. If he was the tough nut who won the ball so fiercely and competitively, Dickinson was the elegant foil. Scoular got his first cap for Scotland against Denmark in October 1951, an honour many thought well overdue.

Portsmouth's middle line equipped them with a backbone and a springboard that enabled them to win the Football League Championship in some style for two consecutive seasons, 1948-49 and 1949-50. It looked as if they would win the FA Cup as well in 1949, when their opponents in the semi-final were Second Division Leicester City but on the day neither Scoular nor Dickinson could subdue Don Revie, then the inspiration of Leicester's attack, and the chance of the Double eluded them. Portsmouth went down 3-1.

Scoular did not miss any of Pompey's league games when they first won the Championship and, when they retained it in 1950 on goal average ahead of Wolves, he missed only half a dozen. Significantly he did not score a single goal in either campaign. In those days that was not seen as being a half-back's job.

From Portsmouth he moved on to an Indian summer with Newcastle United, where he made up for the disappointment of 1949 by playing at Wembley in the FA Cup-winning team that defeated Manchester City 3-1. Altogether he won nine caps for Scotland, though only one of them against England.

On retiring Scoular went into management with Cardiff City, where he did remarkably well with slender resources, not the least of his accomplishments being to stay in office for 10 years. His greatest success was to take the Second Division club all the way to the semi-final of the European Cup-Winners' Cup in 1967-68, beating the powerful Torpedo Moscow in a play-off in the quarter-finals and forcing a draw away to the equally formidable SV Hamburg in the semi-final before losing the return leg 3-2 at Ninian Park.

Jimmy Scoular, born January 11 1925, died March 19 1998

APRIL 24 2004

Lion on his toes

RONNIE SIMPSON

Ronnie Simpson, who has died of a heart attack aged 73, was something of a phenomenon among goalkeepers: a schoolboy wonder who made his first-class debut for the Scottish amateurs Queen's Park at 14 and a resilient veteran still good enough to win major club and international honours in his late 30s, including the European Cup with Celtic in 1967, when he was 36.

His father, Jim Simpson, a famous centre-half for Rangers, was offered the job of trainer at the club. But it was contingent on the understanding that the teenage Ronnie, already showing high promise, would come to Ibrox. Jim Simpson sturdily responded that his son must do as he pleased, and he did not get the job. So the 14-year-old Ronnie made his debut for Queen's Park in a summer cup match against Clyde after playing for his school, King's Park secondary, in the morning. 'I suppose it was the speed of the thing that prevented me being nervous,' he said.

After national service with the Royal Armoured Corps at Catterick he was a member of the British squad in the 1948 Olympic tournament in London. His first professional club was the now defunct Third Lanark but he was there for only six months when he was signed by Newcastle United in February 1951. The incumbent, Jack Fairbrother, looked unassailable but in September broke his collarbone and Ronnie took his place, helping Newcastle to win the FA Cup finals of 1952, against Arsenal, and 1955, against Manchester City.

The Scottish international centre-half Frank Brennan became, he said, a sort of second father to him. 'Though experience can teach you a lot,' Simpson once said, 'the great thing is to keep one's mental reactions sharp all the time.' He did plenty of shouting, he said, and he expected other players to do the same. 'This keeps everyone on their toes.'

In 1960 he returned to Scotland to play 179 games for Hibernian but in the 1963-64 season he was abruptly dropped and never played for the first team again. Disenchanted, he 'lost interest in football', he admitted, but his career then took a remarkable turn. It is generally supposed that Jock Stein, doyen of all Celtic managers, took him back to Glasgow. In fact it seems that Stein, at the time managing Hibs, encouraged Ronnie to join Celtic when their then chief scout, Sean Fallon, came in for him.

Simpson expected merely to be goalkeeping coach and stand-by keeper. Instead he found himself playing with renewed success for the top team, Stein having joined the club as manager and promoted him. As Stein said: 'I don't think Ron is too old at 35, especially the way he is playing. After all, Russia's Yashin is rated best in the world and he's touching 40.'

With Simpson in goal, Celtic became an irresistible power, not only in Scotland but in Europe, with a team made up largely of Glaswegians. Willie Woodburn, who succeeded Jim Simpson as Rangers and Scotland centre-half, would say: 'Ronnie's superb skill and courage laid the foundation for what must be the most successful year in Celtic's long history.'

That year, 1967, was Simpson's *annus mirabilis*. He won the first of his five caps, aged 36, for Scotland, in his team's unexpected victory over England at Wembley and in May he helped Celtic beat Internazionale of Milan in the European Cup final in Lisbon, 2-1. 'I saw less of the ball in that game than probably any other I played in,' he said.

He saw none of it that autumn in Buenos Aires, where Celtic played the second leg of the Intercontinental Cup final against Racing Club. Just before the game he was struck on the head by a missile fired by a catapult from the crowd, was knocked out and forced to leave the field. Celtic, for fear of the riot if they pulled out, played the game and lost 1-0. With the two-leg aggregate tied 2-2 there was a play-off in Montevideo, also shockingly violent, but Stein did not include Simpson, reckoning that, even if he were fit again, he would be in no psychological condition to play.

In October 1971 Simpson became manager of Hamilton Academical in the Scottish Second Division. Later he opened a sports shop in Edinburgh and ran a pub and a post office. In 1970 he had been elected as Progressive councillor in Edinburgh and as late as 1990 he worked as goalkeeping coach with St Johnstone and Partick Thistle.

Ronnie Simpson, born October 11 1930, died April 20 2004

AUGUST 12 2004

Talent to freeze

GORDON SMITH

Gordon Smith, who has died aged 80 after a battle with Alzheimer's disease, was one of the finest Scottish right-wingers, yet his international career was a series of stops and starts, at its best in his veteran years. This was a period in which, first discarded by his principal club Hibernian, then by Hearts – their rivals, whom he had supported as a boy – he reached a dazzling maturity.

Born in Edinburgh but brought up in Montrose, he was a teen-age prodigy, scoring 20 goals in the league tournament of 1941-42. The word was that, with his elegant control, pace and precise crossing, he was going to become 'the Scottish Stanley Matthews' at a time when Matthews was destroying one Scotland left-back after another. Yet, where Matthews had the big-match temperament, Smith proved not to have it at all. He was always a shy person and the international occasion seemed, from his debut at 18 against England, to freeze him and nullify his talents.

Altogether, his way often barred by the more straightforward Willie Waddell of Rangers, he won only 18 full caps over a 10-year period.

After the first half-dozen in the two immediate post-war seasons he did not play for his country again until 1951-52, this despite scoring 25 goals in 29 games in 1949-50.

He was an outstanding member of the 'famous five' Hibs forward line, with Bobby Johnstone, Lawrie Reilly, Eddie Turnbull and Willie Ormond, all internationals. He played 247 Scottish League games for Hibs, scoring 170 goals, helping them to win the title three times. He figured in the Scottish Cup final of 1947 and in the 1951 League Cup final.

Having won the Scottish Championship in 1954-55, in which Smith played 28 games for nine goals, Hibs qualified for the first European Cup, from which Chelsea, under pressure from the insular Football League, withdrew. Smith was still in ebullient form in a team that thrashed Rot Weiss Essen 4-0 in Germany in the first leg of the opening round before drawing at Easter Road 1-1. Djurgarden of Sweden were beaten 3-1 at home, 1-0 away in the quarter-finals but a brilliant Reims team, inspired by Raymond Kopa, eliminated Hibs in the semi-finals, 2-0 in France, 1-0 in Edinburgh.

In the intervening summer Smith had at last regained his place in the Scotland team. Perhaps it was because he felt less pressure playing far from home but he had three exceptional games on tour: a 2-2 draw against Yugoslavia, a handsome 4-1 win against a bruising Austrian team and finally a 3-1 defeat by Hungary in which he had an impressive game. His international record that season was three goals in four games. Half a dozen more appearances, though only one goal, were to come in the next two seasons.

In 1959, after a season in which a recurring ankle injury limited Smith to 15 League games, Hibs gave him a free transfer when they might have been better off paying for the ankle operation, which he paid for himself. So they had to watch him flourish with their City rivals, Hearts, after getting fit on the Riviera. He and Hearts had immediate success, winning Championship and League Cup alike. He scored 10 goals in 29 league games but in the European Cup Hearts lost to Benfica, the eventual winners, in both legs.

In 1961 it was Hearts who let him go to flourish elsewhere, his skill and intelligence making up for lost speed. Again his new club, Dundee, promptly won the Championship, Smith getting seven goals in 32 games. There followed a glorious run in the European Cup, beginning with an 8-1 win over Cologne, though the return was lost 4-0 in Germany. Sporting beat them 1-0 in Lisbon but Dundee won 4-1 in Scotland. However, a 5-1 defeat by Milan, ultimate Cup winners, at San Siro was too much to retrieve, though Dundee won the return 1-0.

Smith retired to live in North Berwick in 1964. For a while in the late 70s he ran a pub near the Hibs ground called the Right Wing. His wife, Joan, predeceased him. He is survived by a son.

Gordon Smith, born May 25 1924, died August 7 2004

DECEMBER 11 2001

Big Ben ban

WILLIE WOODBURN

Willie Woodburn, the former Rangers and Scotland centre-half, who has died aged 82, will be remembered as the player whose successful, if robust, career was cut short by a life ban in September 1954. Though it was lifted some three years later, he was by then 37 and his playing days were virtually at an end.

Always a fiercely uncompromising tackler, he committed the worst of his fouls in retaliation, not least those which led to his draconian suspension. But the severe strictures of the *Glasgow Herald*, after a supposedly friendly match against Denmark, at Hampden Park in May 1951, suggest there was always in Woodburn the potential to go too far. 'We should certainly,' wrote the paper's correspondent, 'cease pointing out the continental faults of pushing and body-checking so long as some of our players are indulging in more serious forms of fouling. If any of our players perpetrates such a foul as Woodburn did in the second half on Saturday, when with a scythe-like sweep of the foot he sent the Danish centre-forward crashing to the ground after the latter had beaten him by skilful footwork, he should be dealt with appropriately.'

Born in Edinburgh, Woodburn attended a school where rugby, not soccer, was played and joined a local junior club called Edinburgh Ashton. Queen's Park, the famous amateur club and owners of Hampden Park, gave him a couple of trials but nothing came of them and he eventually joined Rangers in October 1937. During the war, when Rangers were allowed to field two teams, Woodburn largely played in the lesser of them. But his elegant style, short-stepping and precise in contrast to his powerful tackling, made him clearly a force for the future.

As it transpired, the earlier post-war years saw the central defence position go to big George Young, a player of sharply contrasting style, tall, heavily built and down to earth. The problem was resolved when Young moved to right-back, enabling Woodburn to take his place at centre-half. With such other accomplished Scottish international defenders as Jock Shaw, Ian McColl and Sammy Cox, Rangers embarked on a long spell of domestic success, including two League Championships. Woodburn, with them, would help materially.

Nicknamed 'Big Ben', he won 24 caps for Scotland, the first three in 1946-47, the last four in 1951-52 and five of them in the classic confrontations with England. Had Scotland not sullenly refused to take part in the 1950 World Cup for which they were qualified, he would certainly have played for them in Brazil. Always a perfectionist, he could be hard on his co-defenders if he felt they had failed in their duties.

The fouls and expulsions that brought about his downfall both occurred in games against Stirling Albion. On the first occasion, in 1953, Woodburn retaliated after being punched, was suspended for six weeks and warned by the Scottish FA that 'a very serious view will be taken of any subsequent action'. Rangers lost 2-0 that day.

On August 28 1954, at Ibrox, they reversed the score but Woodburn was expelled after knocking an opponent to the ground. There had been great provocation. Woodburn was carrying a knee injury, exacerbated when an opponent locked his legs around the knee. An exchange of hard words ensued and Woodburn knocked the offender down. So on September 14 came the *sine die* disqualification. It was the fourth time he had been sent off.

Three seasons later the ban was lifted but it was too late. Woodburn became a successful football journalist, much liked and appreciated by his Scottish colleagues.

William Woodburn, born August 8 1919, died December 2 2001

4

Fantasy Five

True to his name

George Best

'If I'd been ugly,' said George Best, who has died aged 59, 'you'd never have heard of Pele.' His dazzling career for Manchester United and Northern Ireland might have lasted as long as Pele's, had his romantic life not taken precedence over his football. Instead his increasingly heavy drinking and womanising caught up with him all too quickly. In his mid-20s, when he should have been moving towards his peak, things went dismally awry. He had retired prematurely and, when he returned to play for Fulham and in Los Angeles, his girth had increased, the dynamic acceleration had gone and the game was deprived of his marvellous virtuosity.

Best was arguably the finest player produced in Britain since the Second World War. He was a compound of almost every talent and another pity of his career is that, though he shone so brightly in the European Cup, he never appeared in the World Cup finals. When it became easier for European teams to qualify, two rather than one team in the eliminating group going through, Best had left the game. Behind him he left an abundance of memories.

For a start, for instance, there was a goal at Old Trafford against Sheffield United in 1971. Picking the ball up on the right, he headed diagonally towards goal, leaving man after man in his wake. Sheffield fans have argued that an injury to a key defender facilitated the goal but who else could have scored it?

More memorable, not least for its significance, was the goal with which he turned the tide in the European Cup final of 1968 at Wembley: Manchester United against Benfica of Lisbon. United, initially ahead, tired towards the end of normal time and seemed in danger of losing. Scarcely had extra-time begun when Best jinked past a defender, tacked outside the keeper and ran the ball into the net. United went on to win with ease, 4-1, the first English team to take the cup.

There were glorious goals, too, in his 37 appearances for Northern Ireland, notably during the Wembley match in 1970 when he spun away from his club colleague, the limpet-like Nobby Stiles, to beat the England keeper, Gordon Banks. He did it in Belfast too, the following year, whipping the ball almost out of Banks's arms before scoring a goal that was dubiously disallowed.

Best was not tall or large, yet there seemed nothing on a football field he could not do. His ball control was exquisite. In a pub he could flip a coin and catch it in his breast pocket. By rights he should have been negligible in the air, yet he could outjump a 6ft defender. Best began as a winger, equally at home on right or left, though chiefly right-footed, yet he developed into a player who could operate across the front line or even in midfield.

Born in Belfast, he was raised on the predominantly Protestant Cregagh estate and played football for the local boys' club and Lisnasharragh Intermediate School. He was hardly out of school when he was snapped up by Manchester United and arrived at Old Trafford in 1961 with his chum, Eric McMordie. Both were so homesick that they fled back to Belfast. McMordie returned to join Middlesbrough while Best was persuaded back to Manchester and put in the care of a motherly landlady, Mary Fullaway.

It might be fair to say that his parental legacy was shaky. Of his natural intelligence, his ebullient humour, there was never any doubt. Those who knew him as a 17-year-old prodigy will remember his modesty and charm. The moustache, the sideburns that he affected in his earlier days with United, might have been seen as a challenge to a more sedate, older generation but he never evinced the louche and loutish behaviour of stars who were to follow.

His First Division debut at Manchester United was made in September 1963 on the wing. The following April he won his first cap for Northern Ireland in Belfast, against Wales. In the 1964-65 season he played a major role in United's capture of the Championship, scoring 10 goals in his 41 games. Another Championship medal would follow in 1966-67 when Best played all 42 games and scored another 10 goals. He would do still better in the following season, with 28 goals in 41.

His finest game, if not the European Cup final of 1968 against Benfica, was probably the time he ran the same club ragged in Lisbon in the same competition in 1966. As Pat Crerand, the tough right-half who was Best's protector in those days, put it: 'Besty just went daft' – but in the most positive way. After six minutes he headed in a free-kick by the United left-back, Tony Dunne. When David Herd headed on a long kick from the keeper, Harry Gregg, Best scored again. Gregg must have been particularly pleased. He was wont to recall playing in a training game against the then unknown Best 'and he done me'. 'This was our finest hour,' said Matt Busby as United ran out winners, 5-1, though the cup eluded them that year.

Best, Denis Law and Bobby Charlton were the stars of a conquering United, though the players tended to divide into camps – Celtic and English. There was never much love lost between Best and the disciplined, conventional Charlton. Once, in a pub, Best threw eggs at a portrait of Charlton.

In 1968 Best was voted European Footballer of the Year and might be seen to have reached his peak, a sublime amalgam of pace, courage, skill, balance and invention.

Off the field, though, his life became increasingly self-indulgent. He drank, gambled and had an infinity of girlfriends –

among them two Miss Worlds and, reportedly, a bride he took upstairs from a hotel bar while his team-mates plied her husband with drink. Busby could do little with him and that little was too late. Best would say later that, when called into Busby's office to be chastised, he would look beyond the manager and count the emblems on the wallpaper. There was a particularly scandalous weekend when he refused to travel with the team to play Chelsea. Instead he spent the weekend in the Islington flat of the actress Sinead Cusack while photographers massed outside.

In 1969 Busby retired but kept an office at Old Trafford, over-shadowing his successors, the former left-half Wilf McGuinness and the former manager of Leicester City Frank O'Farrell. Neither could handle a Best now virtually in freefall. It did not help that, though he continued for a time to play wonderfully well, the team was disintegrating around him. 'My goals became all important because others weren't scoring them so frequently,' he said later. 'Instead of revolving around me the team now depended on me and I lacked the maturity to handle it. I began to drink more heavily and on the field my list of bookings grew longer as my temper grew shorter.'

Sometimes one could hardly blame him. After United met Estudiantes de la Plata in the first leg of the Intercontinental Cup in Buenos Aires in 1968, Best admitted that with a quarter of an hour gone he ceased trying to play because the Argentinians' unceasing, largely unpunished fouls made it impossible. In the return at Old Trafford, his temper snapped and he was sent off.

What could be done? Best built himself a house outside Manchester and failed to turn up for training throughout the first week of 1972. O'Farrell fined him, telling him to stay with his old landlady, Mrs Fullaway, but that could hardly last.

Best said: 'When the bad times started, I couldn't bear the thought of going out on the pitch. I used to drink so I didn't have to think about it. Which came first? The bad times then the drinking or the drinking then the bad times? I'm still sure it was the thought of playing in a bad team, of not winning anything, of not having a chance to play in Europe that drove me to it. All right, you could say that, if I'd trained and lived properly, United might have stood a better chance of doing well. That's true but I just couldn't see myself doing it single-handed.'

Twice Best announced he would retire, twice he changed his mind, but the breaks from training were fatal. He put on weight, which he was never able to lose, and his pace disappeared. His last game for Manchester United was at Queens Park Rangers on New Year's Day, 1974. A spiteful crowd got on his back and a great star was brought low. United lost 3-0.

Now it was downhill all the way. He played a few games for Stockport County and Cork Celtic then, accompanied by his wife Angie, he decamped to the Los Angeles Aztecs. Running along the Californian beach, he observed that people on it might say: 'Who's George Best?' That was in summer 1976. Later that year he went back to England and turned out for Fulham, playing 42 games with eight goals in two seasons. He was slower but still adroit.

Retiring, he became an after-dinner speaker and a television pundit. There were sad, drunken episodes, one of which saw him carted away in a police van and briefly imprisoned. One long-suffering woman after another did her best to care for and reform him but it seldom lasted long.

By March 2000, when liver failure put him in hospital, in much pain, he was married to his second wife, 27-year-old Alex. They divorced in 2004. In July 2002 he had a 10-hour liver transplant operation during which 40 pints of blood was transfused into his body. His glorious footballing days were far distant but his allure remained. He is survived by Calum, the son he had with Angie.

George Best, born May 22 1946, died November 25 2005

FEBRUARY 22 2008

Impish juggler

TOMMY HARMER

Tommy Harmer, who has died aged 79, would doubtless be described today as a cult figure. He was a very special footballer, even a maverick, a triumph of mind over matter and skill over strength. Born in Hackney, east London, the son of a French polisher, he stood only 5ft 6in and weighed a couple of pounds over 9st. When he made his debut for Tottenham Hotspur against Bolton Wanderers in September 1951, the sight of such a tiny, hollow-cheeked, fragile inside-forward, up against the strapping giants of the Bolton defence, prompted fears for his safety.

In no time at all, though, the crowd were marvelling at his cool virtuosity. Surrounded by figures who towered over him, he would juggle with the ball, elude them and send his team on the attack with a perfectly judged pass. With all his sleight of foot, his balance and elusive flair, Harmer was never a player given to 'showboating'. His gifts, complemented by his range of passing, were at the service of the team. Despite being so small, he moved the ball long distances to good effect. He specialised in the devastating through-pass down the middle, on to which the centre-forward could gallop, and he varied this with the crossfield ball to the right wing.

The immediate aftermath of his debut might be seen, in retrospect, as a paradigm of his subsequent career. Nowadays Tottenham players cruise into the car park in their Mercedes and the like. But Harmer, having inspired his team to success and delighted the fans, left squeezed in the back of a modest little car, owned by the correspondent of a local weekly paper.

For all his effectiveness Harmer was always going to find it difficult to hold down a place when Eddie Baily returned from injury. Baily, an England international – which Harmer never became – was a key figure in the 'push and run' set-up favoured by Tottenham at the time under the management of Arthur Rowe. The approach would today be characterised as one-touch, based on the wall pass, and this was emphatically not Harmer's style. He wanted to control the ball, possibly beat an opponent, then pass it long. Thus, although he made 30 appearances in his first two seasons, Baily remained the first choice until he moved on to Nottingham Forest. Only when Rowe departed, Jimmy Anderson succeeded him and, above all, Danny Blanchflower became Spurs' inspiring right-half and captain did Harmer win a regular role.

He with his impishness and the fluent, flamboyant Blanchflower could scarcely have been more different characters but on the field they balanced each other perfectly – both technically accomplished, highly intelligent footballers, given to holding the ball before making shrewd use of it. But by 1959, after the arrival of John White from Falkirk, there was no room for Harmer. When he moved the next year to Watford, then an obscure Third Division team, it seemed a kind of blasphemy. But there he remained, playing regularly for a couple of seasons, before Chelsea rescued him in 1962.

Then aged 34, he played only five times in the side promoted from the Second Division and three games the following season in the First. One of them, dramatically, in February 1964, was at Tottenham, where he took the Spurs defence to pieces. The image remains of him sitting waiflike on the ground, his stocking rolled down to the ankle, putting back his shin pad, but there was nothing waiflike about his performance, which inspired Chelsea to win 2-1. He was like a tiny, mobile signal box, guiding and switching the play. Both Chelsea's goals, by Bobby Tambling, came from

Harmer's passes, the first after 35 seconds, an exquisite chip, to set Tambling free. Yet such skills brought Harmer a single appearance for England B.

At Stamford Bridge, under the volatile Tommy Docherty, he became coach but, when that job came to an end in 1967, the rest was anticlimax. Friends found him a job as a messenger for a London-based Israeli bank. He did not complain; he had never had great expectations. No doubt he would like to have been a member of the Tottenham team which in 1961 became the first of the century to win the Cup and League Double. He had spent most of his career at White Hart Lane, after playing for their amateur, nursery club Finchley, and scored 51 goals for them in 222 appearances.

Thomas Charles Harmer, born February 2 1928, died December 25 2007

OCTOBER 20 2005

Fulham's pass master

JOHNNY HAYNES

Johnny Haynes, who has died aged 71, became a national star as a tiny 15-year-old, playing for England schoolboys in a televised international against Scotland at Wembley half a century ago. Despite his diminutive stature, he commanded the game from inside-left, with precocious passing and neat and elusive control of the ball.

Since he was born in the north-east London suburb of Edmonton it would have seemed natural for Haynes to join Tottenham Hotspur, though his room at home was hung with photographs of

Arsenal players. In the event he joined unfashionable Fulham, the club to which he remained loyal throughout his career. Between Boxing Day 1952 and January 1970 he made 594 league appearances, scored 146 league goals, nine in 43 FA Cup games and two in 20 Football League Cup games. Unquestionably the outstanding influence on the England teams of his day, he received 56 international caps.

A rational perfectionist on the pitch, Haynes became Fulham's most prolific goalscorer but he was famous, above all, for his glorious passing. Whether it was the through-ball to split a defence, the cleverly angled ball inside the back to the left flank or the cross-field pass to the right, he was always the fulcrum of the attack. He did not often bother to beat his man; he let the ball do that.

Before Fulham Haynes served a useful apprenticeship in amateur football all around London, with Feltham, Wimbledon and Woodford Town, in respectively the long-gone Middlesex, Isthmian and Delphian leagues. In January 1954, while on RAF national service, he was a travelling reserve for the first-ever England under-23 team, which lost 3-0 to Italy in Bologna. A year later, at Stamford Bridge, he was the guiding spirit of the side which, scoring five times, took revenge on the Italians. It was only a matter of time before he got a full England cap.

The first of these came in October 1954, against Northern Ireland in Belfast. It was a year before England capped him again, once more against Northern Ireland, but thereafter his place was secure. Until the 1962 World Cup, when he captained England in a losing quarter-final against Brazil in Vina del Mar, Haynes missed only eight of England's 63 games – and for half of those he was chosen despite Fulham being a Second Division club.

He would surely have won more caps but later in 1962, driving at night along the Blackpool front after a First Division game, he was involved in an accident that left his knee severely damaged.

He fought his way back to play for Fulham but was never again called up by England, though he was still only 31 when England won the 1966 World Cup.

In truth Haynes was not at his best in either the 1958 or 1962 World Cups, in which he did take part. In Sweden, in 1958, he was plainly weary. Fulham had been involved in memorable battles both in the league and in the FA Cup, in which they were knocked out in a semi-final replay by a Manchester United team patched together after the Munich air disaster. Haynes had been in his best form that day, breaking up United's attacks and setting his own forwards on the move. In the 38th minute he began the movement which ended with Jimmy Hill shooting past Harry Gregg to put Fulham 2-1 into the lead.

But for England, in Sweden, Haynes was seldom at his peak. He did produce, against Brazil in Gothenburg, one memorable through-pass, which might have decided the game but the final score was 0-0 and England eventually went out to Russia. (A few months later, at Wembley, Haynes took a kind of revenge, scoring three times against the Russians, with tremendous left-footed shots from outside the penalty area.)

The following year, 1958-59, Haynes captained Fulham back to the First Division. He also became the first major beneficiary of the abolition of the maximum wage rule – a move masterminded by his old partner Hill, then chairman of the players' union – and his salary rose to an undreamed of £100 a week. He captained England, somewhat abrasively, in the 1962 World Cup finals, which were again a disappointment.

On retirement in 1970 Haynes, already an active bookmaker, played in South Africa for Durban City. Fifteen years later, having sold his chain of bookmakers' shops to the Tote in 1976, he settled in Edinburgh, where he played a great deal of golf.

For all his undoubted gifts, Haynes was a controversial player for both club and country. The chief criticism of him as an international was that his football was somewhat stereotyped and thus quite possible to predict and counter. At Fulham it was sometimes said that he was too overwhelming, even inhibiting, a figure, though his contribution and loyalty to the club were immense. He was a sometimes impatient but undeniably gifted perfectionist. Curiously, for so assured and dominant a figure, he never had any ambitions to become a manager. He is survived by his wife, Avril.

John Norman Haynes, born October 17 1934, died October 18 2005

FEBRUARY 24 2000

Wizard of dribble

SIR STANLEY MATTHEWS

Stanley Matthews, who has died aged 85, was the first European Footballer of the Year and arguably the outstanding British player of his generation. He was nicknamed the Wizard of Dribble in Britain and was known abroad as Der Zauberer, the magician.

His career stretched from well before the Second World War to the 1960s and he was still playing League football at 50. At 41, at Wembley, he was capable of demolishing as famous a left-back as Brazil's Nilton Santos. Afterwards, in the England dressing room, in a rare moment of spleen, he said that when he read that he was too old he was sometimes tempted to tear up the paper.

The truth is that throughout his career Matthews was accused of being too this, that or the other: too unpredictable, too individualistic, too slow to release the ball. In one wartime Wembley international there was a small scandal when it was alleged that he had been deliberately starved of the ball and at the end of the war, when football officially restarted, he was excluded from the England team for most of the 1946-47 season in favour of Tom Finney, an outside-right with almost as remarkable a body swerve. But he returned in triumph in Lisbon, Matthews on the right, Finney on the left, Portugal 0 England 10.

As early as November 1934, when England won the bruising Battle of Highbury against an Italian team which ran amok when its Argentinian captain, Luisito Monti, limped early off the field with a broken foot, Matthews was damned in the *Daily Mail*. Geoffrey Simpson, its sports columnist, wrote: 'I saw Matthews play just as moderately in the recent inter-League match, exhibiting the same slowness and hesitation. Perhaps he lacks the big-match temperament.'

Matthews was born at Hanley in the Potteries, third son of a formidable boxer, Jack Matthews, 'the Fighting Barber of Hanley'. Jack encouraged all his four boys to keep physically fit, doing deep breathing exercises in front of an open window even on the coldest mornings. In later years Matthews would devise his own regimes based on long runs across the Blackpool beaches. It used to be said that, if you passed his house at 9pm, the lights of his bedroom would be out.

His swerve was something which defied analysis just as it defied attempts to counter it. He would take the ball up to the opposing left-back who, even if he were mentally prepared for it, would still buy the dummy when Matthews swayed slightly to the left, putting the opponent off balance, only to wriggle round to the right, flick the ball up the touchline with the outside of his right foot and sprint away. Catch him if you could. Over those vital first 10 yards or so, he was beyond pursuit. 'Don't ask me how I do it,' he once said of the swerve. 'It just comes out of me under pressure.'

'You must have butterflies,' he would say – butterflies in the stomach, he meant, before a game, building up adrenalin, anticipation. And he still had them in the dressing room before his comeback game for Stoke City in 1961, a mere Second Division match, aged 46.

Having sped past his left-back and reached the goal-line, Matthews would pull the ball back into the goalmouth, the most effective pass in the game. He seldom scored himself but he could do so when necessary, as he showed when playing at Tottenham for England against Czechoslovakia in 1937. Injury had reduced England to 10 fit men and their unbeaten home record against foreign teams seemed in jeopardy. Matthews, moving to inside-right, scored three times and England won 5-4.

Much later, in the 1954 World Cup in Switzerland, when England were struggling in their opening game against Belgium, Matthews moved to inside-forward, galvanised the team and helped them gain a 4-4 draw.

Over the years he would repeatedly fall foul of the England selectors, troubled by so maverick a talent. It is true that he began badly, at 19, in his first two internationals against Wales and Italy, but it was not long before the 'big-match temperament' was asserting itself.

In May 1939, in the Berlin Olympic Stadium, he had one of his finest games for England when they needed it most. Forced to give the Nazi salute before they played the German international side, England cut them to ribbons, with Matthews rampant, irresistible against a full-back who had played him out of the game when the teams had last met. Reinhold Muenzenberg could do nothing with him that day and England won 6-3.

An outstanding schoolboy footballer, Matthews once scored a dozen goals in a game from centre-half. He played for England schoolboys, joined his local club Stoke City straight from school, worked in the office and made his league debut for them soon after he had turned 17. But even before the war his relations with the club degenerated with the appointment as manager of Bob McGrory, a former Stoke defender. It has been suggested that McGrory was displeased by Matthews replacing his friend, Bobby Liddle, on the right wing. Relations did not improve when Matthews returned to Stoke after the war.

During it he had played as a guest for Blackpool, a town where he and his wife, Betty, had opened a small hotel. Things came to a climax early in the 1946-47 season when Matthews was kept out of the Stoke team by the young winger, George Mountford. Eventually Stoke agreed to transfer him to Blackpool, for £11,500. Matthews would stay there happily, forming famous wing partnerships with Stan Mortensen and Jackie Mudie, until his romantic and belated return to Stoke, in 1961.

The war ate up much of his 'official' career but he found an ideal partner in the England team in Sunderland's Raich Carter, even though Carter once complained that, when he gave Matthews the ball, he never got it back. Tactfully his captain, Stanley Cullis, responded that having passed he should move into the middle. The England attack, which included Tommy Lawton and Denis Compton, was an outstanding one, with an 8-0 win over Scotland at Maine Road, Manchester, to its credit.

Losing, then regaining, his place in the England team in the first official post-war season, 1946-47, Matthews excelled in Lisbon against Portugal and, a year later in Turin, reduced poor, blond Alberto Eliani, standing in as Italy's left-back for Virgilio Maroso, to tatters. England won 4-0.

But when it came to Cup finals, a winner's medal persistently eluded Matthews. In the 1948 final Blackpool lost 4-2 to Manchester United, despite taking the lead through Eddie Shimwell's penalty. In 1951 two spectacular goals by Jackie

Milburn enabled Newcastle United to win 2-0. It seemed that 1953 would almost surely be the last chance. Blackpool were to meet Bolton and this time luck favoured them when Eric Bell, left-half and thus a direct opponent for Matthews, was hurt and had to limp on the left-wing.

Even then Blackpool made heavy weather of it. They conceded an absurd early goal when their Scottish international goalkeeper, George Farm, misjudged a shot by Nat Lofthouse after 75 seconds. Lofthouse hit the post, Bell tore a muscle and Bolton were already down to 10 active men.

Stan Mortensen would later say that Bolton lost the game when they moved their English international left-winger Bobby Langton inside rather than let him contest space with Matthews on the wing. Blackpool's equaliser, 10 minutes from the break, was a fluke, the ball going in off their emergency left-half, Harold Hassall. But Bolton gallantly hit back with two goals, one by Willie Moir, with Farm at fault again, the second a brave header by Bell himself. There were only 20 minutes left.

It was now that Matthews, strangely obscure till then, came into the game. Ralph Banks, Bolton's left-back, was exhausted by his efforts to halt Matthews, contracting cramp in his shins and four times leaving the field for treatment in the final quarter-hour. A Matthews cross which would have gone out of play had Stan Hanson not flapped at it, reached Mortensen on the far post and he made it 3-2 before equalising breathlessly from a free-kick.

Then, classically, Matthews got away again, beat Banks, took the ball up to the centre-half, Malcolm Barrass, and pulled back an exquisite cross, not to Mortensen but to the South African left-winger Bill Perry, free on the far post. A right-footed shot gave Blackpool the Cup and the match its name, 'the Matthews Final'.

Before then, in 1950, England had suffered the most humiliating defeat in their history, defeat by the United States at Belo

Horizonte in the World Cup. It will never be known if Matthews would have prevented it. It was only at the last moment that he was grudgingly recalled to the squad at all. He did play the last game, lost against Spain in Rio 1-0, but the die was cast by then.

Matthews' long marriage to Betty ended in 1968. He remarried, this time to a Czech linguist, Mila Winter, cultural assistant at the US embassy. He and Betty had two children, Jean and Stanley Jr. The latter was three times British junior tennis champion, as well as Wimbledon boys champion in 1962, but never quite fulfilled his early promise and eventually turned to coaching in the US.

Knighted in 1965, a month before his 50th birthday, Stanley Matthews altogether made 698 appearances in the Football League for 71 goals and played 54 full internationals for England for 11 goals. In 1963 he had the great satisfaction of helping Stoke City regain the First Division.

A period as manager of Port Vale, after Stoke had sullenly parted company with him, reducing his wages and refusing him complimentary tickets, was ill-starred. The club fell foul of regulations concerning the signing of young players and Matthews was unfairly found culpable.

He went on to live in Malta, where he played for Hibernians at 55, and to coach widely abroad, especially in South Africa, where he had first worked in 1954, and in Canada, before returning to the Potteries. His wife Mila died last year.

Sir Stanley Matthews, born February 1 1915, died February 23 2000

NOVEMBER 29 2000

Clown Prince

LEN SHACKLETON

Len Shackleton, who has died aged 78, called his autobiography *Clown Prince of Soccer*. It became famous for a chapter headed The Average Director's Knowledge of Football and consisting of a blank page. Shackleton, a perennial maverick and enormously gifted inside-forward, won only five caps for England and was eternally 'agin the government'.

The roots of his dissent may be found in his experiences as an Arsenal apprentice just before the Second World War. A Yorkshireman, he was spotted by Arsenal, brought down to London and parked at their nursery club at Enfield. 'This then frail boy' was how a match programme described him during the war. Those words were probably written by George Allison, Arsenal's orotund manager, who offended Shackleton irremediably when he called him in to say the club was letting him go. Allison showed off the television set in his office, a rarity then. Far from being grateful or impressed, Shackleton reacted bitterly – the provincial yokel condescendingly being shown a marvel of new technology.

So 'Shack' returned to Bradford, where he was born, signed for Bradford Park Avenue and, during the war, went into the mines as a Bevin boy. He continued to play for the club and made a big impression as a gifted all-round attacker.

Arms slightly akimbo in his characteristic stance, a master of ball control, a maker of jewelled passes and often a scorer himself, he was first picked for England in a victory international against Scotland, in 1946, at Hampden. It did not turn out well for

Shackleton. England lost 1-0 and it was he who gave away the free-kick that let Jimmy Delaney score the Scottish goal. Shack did not play for England again until September 1948, in a goalless draw in Copenhagen.

Between times big clubs circled him and Newcastle United got him. In 1946 they paid Bradford City the huge sum of £13,000 and he made a spectacular debut at Gallowgate. Newcastle beat Newport County 13-0 in a Second Division game and Shackleton scored six of them. That season Newcastle were not only promoted but they also reached the Cup semi-finals.

But Shack did not stay long at Newcastle. He relates in his book how a director told him, more or less, to box clever, implying that, were he to accept a transfer, there would be money in it for him. Before 1947 was out he had made the short move to Wearside and Sunderland.

Though Sunderland never won anything of consequence in those years, their expensively assembled team played much fine football. Shackleton teamed up with another gifted player, the Londoner Ivor Broadis, though his relations with the powerful Welsh international centre-forward, Trevor Ford, were less happy. Shackleton took a malign delight in giving Ford what appeared to be perfect passes which, in fact, had such a fiendish bias on them that the ball was impossible to control – back-spun chips that defied mastery. Once, during a friendly in Holland, he dribbled through the whole of the opposing defence, finally rolling the ball back to Ford in the goal-mouth with a cry of 'Don't say I never give you a pass'.

Despite his talents he was too idiosyncratic for a regular place in the England team, where it was always important that the face should fit. It is told that once, when he was training with the England squad, Walter Winterbottom, the pedagogic England manager, said: 'I want all you five forwards to run down the field, interpassing the ball, until you come to the goal, where there'll be no goalkeeper. Then put the ball into the net.' Shackleton, lying on the ground, looked up sardonically: 'Which side of the net, Mr Winterbottom?' he inquired.

By coincidence the only three caps he won in the British international tournament were all against Wales, in 1948, 1949 and 1954. He never figured in a national World Cup squad. Probably his finest game was at Wembley in the autumn of 1954, against West Germany, who had just won the World Cup in Switzerland. Stricken by jaundice, they had a weakened team. England, by contrast, were strengthened by the withdrawal of several regulars, obliging them to pick a brilliant side of ball players, of whom Shackleton was one. In a 3-1 victory, obtained with much fine football, his goal was the *pièce de résistance*. Luring the German keeper out of goal, he beat him with an exquisite chip. But 1954 would be the last year that he played for England, though he was only 32.

He was, however, no rolling stone. Sunderland, who had paid what seemed then a whopping £20,500 for him, kept him for the rest of his career, which ended with a single appearance in the 1957-58 Championship. Only three times did he get into double figures as a league goalscorer but, in his best season, 1951-52, he scored 22 goals in 41 appearances.

For Bradford he had played only seven 'official' games in the Second Division, scoring four goals, before he went to Newcastle but, of course, there were many appearances for Bradford during the war. Altogether Shackleton played 384 league games for 126 goals.

While playing for Sunderland, he opened a barber's shop in the town. On retirement he became a sports journalist. He moved to Grange-over-Sands, in Cumbria, and suffered a heart attack in August. He had recently completed *Return of the Clown Prince*, with his son Roger, who survives him, as do his wife, Marjorie, and two other sons.

Leonard Francis Shackleton, born May 13 1922, died November 28 2000

5

Grand
Miscellany

Cut short by Munich

JACKIE BLANCHFLOWER

Jackie Blanchflower, who has died of cancer aged 65, spent most of his 25th birthday asleep in a hospital bed in Munich. Cheerful nuns and nurses woke him to sing Happy Birthday. It was hardly that, though he was touched by the gesture. A month earlier, on February 6 1958, Blanchflower had been one of the seriously injured survivors of the air crash that killed eight Manchester United players on their way back from a European Cup match against Red Star Belgrade.

Jackie, the team's elegant, adventurous centre-half, and Northern Ireland's too, had suffered a broken right arm, which would give him pain for a long while to come, and a fractured pelvis. Those injuries forced him to retire from the game and he never played again. But he took up a career in accountancy and was a popular after-dinner speaker. Just two weeks ago he attended a memorial match at Old Trafford which raised funds for crash survivors.

It is slightly ironic he should outlive by several years his older brother, Danny, whose career overshadowed his own. As right-half and captain of Spurs and Northern Ireland, Danny was outstanding among the players of his day, not only a skilful footballer but an eloquent one too, writing columns for, among others, the *New Statesman*.

But no one was more aware than Danny of his younger brother's virtues, nor more disappointed that Jackie's significant presence was denied the Northern Ireland team which, four months after Munich, was due to figure for the first time in the

World Cup finals in Sweden. The loss of Jackie, Danny observed, meant that Northern Ireland's tactics were radically affected. Jackie, a 'footballing' centre-half, clever on the ball and constructive in his use of it, was self-reliant enough to allow Danny, the team's right-half, to play well upfield, largely in a creative role. With Jackie gone, and a full-back put into the centre-half position to fill the breach, Danny was obliged to play a much more cautious and protective role.

Danny had also been full of praise for his brother's versatile performance in the 1957 FA Cup final at Wembley, for Manchester United against Aston Villa, when United's goalkeeper, Ray Wood, was injured and forced to play most of the match hobbling on the wing. Jackie went into goal and performed with great agility and aplomb. Not only did he save shots, all but two, but, as Danny emphasised, his use of the ball when he had it, always throwing it to a team-mate rather than belting it upfield, was exemplary.

Born in Belfast, Jackie joined United as a wing-half and operated for a time as an inside-forward. But his one failing, a lack of pace, led to his dropping back, in due course, to centre-half. In 1954 he made his debut for Northern Ireland against Wales, going on to win a dozen caps. At United he had a rival for the centre-half position in Mark Jones, a solid and more orthodox defender who, alas, perished at Munich. Blanchflower, however, was just as dominant in the air, and a good deal more resourceful on the ground. Besides his role in United's early European Cup adventures he won a League Championship medal with them in 1955-56. He is survived by his wife, Jean.

Jackie Blanchflower, born March 7 1933, died September 2 1998

SEPTEMBER 9 2005

Thinking man's full-back

NOEL CANTWELL

Noel Cantwell, who has died aged 73, was one of the best full-backs of his generation, with West Ham United, with Manchester United and with the Irish international team. He guided Manchester United to the FA Cup in 1963 and was a double international, representing his country at both football and cricket. Tall, handsome and well built, he was ever fluent and humorous.

Cantwell was born in Cork and emerged with the local team, Cork Athletic. In the second half of 1952-53 he went to east London, making three league appearances for West Ham United before, the following season, gaining a regular place with 22 appearances. That season also saw him win the first of 36 international caps for the Republic of Ireland.

He was a committed and intelligent thinker about the game, so West Ham was the ideal club for him. There at that time were Malcolm Allison, later an outstanding coach with Manchester City and Crystal Palace, then a centre-half, and Phil Woosnam, a Welsh international inside-forward with a BSc degree, a background in school teaching and subsequently a leading role in the development of professional football in the United States. These three were mentors of the young Bobby Moore.

Essentially a left-back, though versatile enough in the years after he had moved, in 1960-61, to represent Ireland at centre-forward, Cantwell was a strong header of the ball, an excellent positional player and – in days before the four-man defence and overlapping full-back – always eager to move upfield and have a crack at goal. He scored 16 league goals for West Ham and another 19 for Manchester United. At corners he never liked to stay on the post but, given his heading, preferred to be able to attack the kick as it came in.

For West Ham, between 1953 and 1960, he made 245 League appearances, 33 of them when the club were promoted from the Second Division in 1957-58 when he got four league goals. He had a notable partnership with John Bond at right-back.

With Manchester United he made 121 league appearances and was at left-back when they beat Leicester City 3-1 in the FA Cup final of 1963. Winning his first Irish cap in 1953, he got the last in 1966-67. He had 14 international goals to his name.

Retiring from the game in 1967, when he seemed able to continue to play successfully at the top level, Cantwell became manager of Coventry City, a club that at that time clung uneasily to its First Division status. Indeed, in the first of his five seasons there Cantwell saved them from relegation by a single point but in 1969 they emerged as one of the more promising teams in the First Division.

In 1972 he became manager of Peterborough United, where he stayed for five years winning the Fourth Division Championship and promotion in 1972-73. He had a second managerial spell at Peterborough between 1986 and 1988, after which he continued for a time as the club's general manager, making his home in the city. There, in 1991, he opened a pub. To his delight he was more recently enlisted by England's Swedish manager Sven-Goran Eriksson to go scouting for him, reporting on potential England players.

An accomplished all-round sportsman, he played seven times for Ireland's cricket team and, after Essex representatives watched him making 47 runs against the New Zealanders, was asked to join that county. Cantwell turned this down, saying he did not want to spend his whole year in England.

During a five-year spell in the United States, with the Boston and Jacksonville professional teams, he won the Eastern Division Championship of the North American Soccer League in 1978 with the New England Teamen.

His family life was cruelly blighted when his 22-year-old son, one of his three children, was killed in a car crash.

Noel Cantwell, born February 28 1932, died September 8 2005

FEBRUARY 18 2004

Miller's tale

HENRY COCKBURN

There could scarcely have been a sharper physical contrast than that between two famous Manchester United left-halves – little Henry Cockburn, who has died aged 80, and the massive Duncan Edwards, who succeeded him in 1953. Both played with much success for England but, whereas Cockburn was 5ft 6in tall, weighed little more than 10st, relied on speed of thought and foot and was, under the circumstances, astonishingly good in the air, Edwards had the added advantage of muscular power.

Cockburn was born in Ashton-under-Lyne, Lancashire, and played for an amateur team called Goslings before joining United on amateur forms in 1943, turning professional a few weeks before his 21st birthday, having played as a guest for Accrington Stanley.

By the end of the Second World War he had a regular place in United's Northern League team, so the fact that he had played only six First Division games before making his England debut, against Wales in October 1946, was irrelevant. It was the first of his 13 caps and he was still working in a local mill.

He was certainly the outstanding member of a United half-back line that had the forceful Allenby Chilton in the middle and the diligent John Anderson on the right. In 1949 a journalist eulogised Cockburn as 'one of the most astute ball players in the game today' while critics marvelled at the heights he leapt to win headers.

Cockburn won three caps in that first post-war season but did not return to the England team until 1948. He was a salient member of the United team that beat Blackpool 4-2 at Wembley in a scintillating FA Cup final, he helped England defeat Scotland 2-0 at Hampden and in May he was a prominent member of the side that trounced Italy 4-0 in Turin.

Cockburn won five more caps the following season but there was then a two-year gap before, in May 1951, he was recalled to Wembley to help England beat Argentina 2-1. He earned his last cap in 1952, in a 2-2 draw against France at Highbury. In the 1951-52 season he also had the satisfaction of winning the League Championship with Manchester United, their first such victory since 1911. Altogether he played 275 league matches for United, all in the First Division, though he scored only four goals.

A turning point came in October 1953, in a friendly game at Kilmarnock, when midway through the first half Cockburn had to leave the field injured and was replaced by the 17-year-old Edwards. He never recovered his regular place and, in October 1954, was transferred to Bury for £3,000. Further transfers took him to Peterborough United in July 1956, non-league Corby Town in July 1959 and Sankey's FC (Wellington) in December 1960.

Two months later, however, he embarked on a successful new career, as assistant trainer at Oldham until September 1964, when he moved to Huddersfield Town as assistant trainer-coach, then senior coach from 1965 to 1975.

Henry Cockburn, born September 14 1923, died February 2 2004

Keeping it safe for Spurs

TED DITCHBURN

Ted Ditchburn, who has died aged 84, was one of the outstanding goalkeepers of the 1940s and 50s, tall and well-built, fearless, acrobatic and a long-range kicker. But for all the excellence of his extensive and successful career with Spurs, his temperament continually betrayed him when he played for England and not until his veteran years did he finally conquer it, giving at international level the performances he had long turned in for Tottenham.

Born in Gillingham, Kent, the son of a professional boxer, Ditchburn had the sort of huge hands that once seemed likely to be dedicated to the ring, until he changed his mind. Fellow footballers were ill-advised to spar with him in the dressing-room. Even Jack Chisholm, Tottenham's massive centre-half, recalled going out on the field once somewhat dizzy after a brief exchange with Ditchburn, all in good fun but nonetheless confusing.

Ditchburn first played for Spurs in their Second Division side in the unfinished 1939-40 season. Then he joined the RAF, with which, at one point, he was posted to Burma. His prowess in the Tottenham goal led to his being picked for England in a wartime international at Wembley in 1944, a time when Frank Swift seemed an automatic selection. His first full cap came in late 1948 when, at Highbury, England put out a much changed team against

Switzerland and won 6-0. The following May, in Stockholm, Ditchburn had another chance, as Swift's international career came to a close, but his anxieties betrayed him. He had a shaky game, Sweden won 3-1 and the England succession went to Wolverhampton Wanderers' Bert Williams.

Consolation came in his seasons with Spurs. In that summer of 1949 Arthur Rowe took over the team, introduced his innovative push-and-run tactics and signed Alf Ramsey from Southampton. Nicknamed the General, Ramsey immediately became the largest influence on the team, not least because of his understanding with Ditchburn. Where goalkeepers had long been accustomed, when they took the ball, to boot it long and hard up the field, Ramsey would pass back to Ditchburn, or the keeper would throw it to Ramsey, and an attack would be built up from there.

It was a tactic that had its perils. In May 1951 during a so-called Festival of Britain match at Tottenham against German opposition, Ditchburn moved out of goal to claim a pass back from Ramsey and a German forward, lunging at the ball, broke his finger. Fortunately the episode did not stop Ditchburn from taking part in every league game the following season.

His appearance record was, indeed, remarkable. In the first two post-war league seasons in the Second Division he did not miss a match. In the next five league seasons he played all 42 games – including throughout Tottenham's promotion season of 1949-50, when they won the Second Division title, and 1950-51, when they won the Championship. Altogether Ditchburn made 418 league appearances for Spurs, a club record until 1975, the last couple coming in 1958-59.

The Indian summer of his international career arrived in 1956-57, though in the interim he had made only one appearance, in June 1953 in New York, when he was reserve goalkeeper on an American tour. He let through three goals, though England scored six. In 1956, however, at the age of 35, he was playing so well for Spurs that he was recalled to the England goal, appearing against Wales, Yugoslavia and Denmark, taking his total number of caps to six, a somewhat meagre reward given his consistent excellence at club level. He then spent six years at non-league Romford.

On retirement he opened a sports shop in the town and then ran a newsagent's not far from White Hart Lane. He is survived by his wife, Joan, whom he married in 1943, and his son, Robin. His daughter, Christine, predeceased him.

Edwin George Ditchburn, born October 24 1921, died December 26 2005

JUNE 5 1999

Whistling brewer

ARTHUR ELLIS

Arthur Ellis, who has died aged 84, has his place in football history as the gallant referee of a notoriously violent World Cup game, between Brazil and Hungary in the 1954 quarter-finals, the 'Battle of Berne'.

Referees were years short of being full-time then. Ellis, Halifax-born, earned his living as a brewery representative. He had cut his teeth on Yorkshire junior soccer, then steadily worked his way on to the Football League list.

Four years before the Battle of Berne he had officiated at two significant matches in Brazil. First Sweden surprised Italy 3-2; then in the final pool, in one of the most spectacular performances of any World Cup, Sweden, outplayed by the Brazilian attack, lost 7-1.

It was the Brazilians who instigated the trouble in Berne. 'The adoption of a defensive system, borrowed from an alien environment,' wrote the football historian Jerry Weinstein, 'repressed their natural talent and brought about their downfall. The resulting frustration contributed greatly towards their fury, which was released in the match against Hungary.' He was referring to the third-back game, never truly assimilated in Brazil.

After only three minutes Nandor Hidegkuti, trying to connect with a corner, had his shorts torn off. It rained heavily, the pitch was muddy, Hungary went two up and, as Weinstein wrote: 'Some of the tackling might have been excused but it degenerated from the harsh to the brutal, from the attempt to get the ball to the effort at stopping the man who had it.'

The sturdy Ellis would have none of it. In the second half, when a magnificent goal by the right-winger, Julinho, reduced Brazil's deficit to 2-3, things became more heated. Jozef Bozsik, the talented Hungarian right-half and a member of parliament, and Nilton Santos, the usually cool Brazilian left-back, came to blows and Ellis had no hesitation in sending them both off. (When he came across Bozsik at another game and asked whether he had been sanctioned, the player said: 'In Hungary we do not punish members of parliament.')

Brazil's trainer came on the field after the double expulsion to berate Ellis, who summoned policemen to hustle the man away. As things continued to deteriorate, Ellis could do little about the mayhem behind his back but four minutes from time he expelled a second Brazilian, the inside-left Humberto Tozzi, for kicking an opponent. In the circumstances of the game, which Hungary won 4-2, Ellis seemed almost restrained. Without his control it would hardly have been finished.

An Italian critic described his refereeing as 'magisterial'. In Brazil he was excoriated. Ellis himself remarked calmly: 'The laws of the game are the same all over the world. I carry them out to the best of my ability. I could take no other action than I did.' He described the match as 'one of the most disgusting exhibitions witnessed'.

Later he took his wife Kathleen, who died in 1987, and two young sons, Ian and Duncan, to Switzerland. The boys had tickets for Brazil v Yugoslavia at Lausanne, where Ellis was on the line. They got in but he and the Scottish referee, Charlie Faultless, had to argue for a quarter of an hour before they could enter, having forgotten their official passes.

During the game, with Brazil one down, one of their players kicked the ball into touch. Their trainer promptly threw back a smaller ball, such as his team preferred. Ellis immediately ordered the original ball to be given back.

After retiring at the compulsory age of 47 he found fame on the TV programme It's a Knockout, again as referee, and for more than 30 years was chairman of the Pools Panel, adjudicating on postponed matches.

He once told of the time when out of the goodness of his heart he gave a talk to a small Lancashire football club. Afterwards he sat down to a 'comforting little meal' of hotpot. As he was walking away, the club secretary came panting after him. 'Mr Ellis,' he said, 'you forgot to pay us for the 'otpot.'

Arthur Ellis, born July 8 1914, died May 23, 1999

August 11 2003

Coach who listened

Ray Harford

Ray Harford, who has died from cancer aged 58, was famous for his prowess as a football coach though he was less successful as a manager. However, it should not be forgotten what an outstanding job he made of managing Luton Town, leading them to a sensational victory over Arsenal, 3-2, with a dramatic late burst of goals in the 1988 final of the Football League Cup at Wembley.

To show it was no fluke he got Luton to the final again the following year, though this time they lost 3-1 to Nottingham Forest after holding a 1-0 lead at half-time. He was sacked a year later by a chairman who accused him of being humourless and dour. Anyone who knew Harford would fail to recognise the description. He was a man of charm, humour and geniality.

He was born in Halifax simply because his mother happened to have been evacuated there. Soon they were back in her native Bermondsey. He was much amused in later years when, after a match in which he scored the winning goal at the Shay Stadium against Halifax Town, a local journalist wrote that Halifax had been defeated by one of their own.

Standing 6ft 1in and weighing just under 13st, Harford was a centre-half whose playing career never quite took off. Charlton Athletic signed him as a teenager but he passed on to Exeter City, Lincoln City, Mansfield, Port Vale and Colchester United. It was at Colchester in 1975 that he joined the coaching staff, which was the start of an impressive career.

The concept of the coach was virtually unknown in British football until well after the Second World War. A coach's position is tantalisingly ambiguous. Often when things go well for a club you hear that he, rather than the manager, has been behind it. But managers shelter and protect coaches, who do not always do so well when they find themselves blinking in the daylight. This happened to Harford in his appointment at Blackburn Rovers.

He came as coach in 1991 and, as his manager, Kenny Dalglish, readily conceded, played a leading part in the team's winning of the 1994-95 Premier League title. Dalglish did not coach and did not want to but, when he kicked himself upstairs to become chief executive, all Jack Walker's money could not save Harford from disaster and he went soon afterwards.

Colin Hendry, the Scottish international centre-half of that Blackburn side, remembered Harford as a 'top-class coach, who was very influential in my career. A nice man who was always ready to lend an ear.' That is very much the way he is remembered at Millwall, where he held his last position as coach.

After last Saturday's home match against Wigan the Millwall manager, Mark McGhee, said: 'He was very proud of his boys. He was like an uncle to them. He was more than a coach. The boys were younger when Ray came here and they developed with him. He'd have been upset if we lost.' The one minute's silence by the Millwall fans, in Harford's honour, was impeccable.

In 1981 he had become youth coach at Fulham and he was promoted the following year to first-team coach under Malcolm Macdonald's managership. But those were difficult days for Fulham, whose chairman, Ernie Clay, was hell-bent on breaking up the team and selling Craven Cottage. Harford became manager in 1984 but could not stop the club sliding into the Third Division.

After Luton Wimbledon made him first coach in 1990, then manager but he never seemed at ease there and he was off to Blackburn the next year. More recently he had coached at Queens

Park Rangers and West Bromwich Albion. It was the thing he did best. He is survived by his wife, Maureen, and son, Paul.

Ray Harford, born June 1 1945, died August 9, 2003

FEBRUARY 21 2003

Pompey flyer

PETER HARRIS

In the late 1940s and early 1950s, when Portsmouth were such a power in football, few made a greater contribution to that ebullient team than Peter Harris, who has died aged 77. An outside-right in the classical tradition, he was fast, well balanced and elusive. Portsmouth won the Championship in the 1948-49 and 1949-50 seasons and were favoured to do the 1949 League and Cup Double, only to be beaten in a Highbury semi-final by Second Division Leicester City.

Under the shrewd managership of the club's former chief scout Bob Jackson Pompey surpassed themselves in the 1948-49 season, winning the title five points ahead of Manchester United, with all five forwards achieving double figures in goals. Of these Harris, with 17, was equal top with the big, powerful Duggie Reid. The following season, with Portsmouth champions again, Harris played in 40 of the 42 matches, scoring 16 goals, one fewer than the top scorer, Ike Clarke. Pompey this time won the title only on goal average, at the expense of Wolves.

Born in Portsmouth, close to the Fratton Park ground, Harris was adept at cutting in to score. Portsmouth made profitable use of their two wingers. Harris played on the right, standing 5ft 7in and weighing only 10st 2lb. Jack Froggatt, the muscular, blond left-winger, stood 5ft 8in but weighed over 12st, a build that enabled him to play also as a centre-half.

Harris would be capped only twice over almost a five-year period for England and on each occasion the game ended disastrously for the national team, though Harris himself was hardly to blame. In 1949 an early-season match at Goodison Park against the Republic of Ireland saw England defeated 2-0, though they fielded a somewhat experimental team. It was the first defeat by a team from outside Great Britain, though that distinction would subsequently, albeit wrongly, be given to the 1953 Hungarian side because they did it at Wembley. It was against these same Hungarians, in May 1954, that Harris was surprisingly recalled to an England side which lost 7-1. He never won another cap.

Portsmouth and Harris would not win the League again but they remained strong contenders, finishing fourth in 1951-52 and third in 1954-55. Perhaps Pompey had been living above their means for in 1959 they, and Harris, fell into the Second Division after a season in which they gave away 112 goals and ended nine points adrift. Nonetheless, in an era when the maximum wage imposed a rough equality, Portsmouth and their locally nurtured players had their place in the sun.

In 1960 Harris was forced to retire with tuberculosis. He convalesced in Hayling Island and then managed a restaurant complex. Later he ran the Portsmouth former championship XI for charity and worked with handicapped children. Last year an auction of his mementoes raised £14,000. He is survived by his wife, Sylvia. They had no children.

Peter Harris, born December 19 1925, died January 5 2003

NOVEMBER 10 2004

Captain Crazy Horse

EMLYN HUGHES

Emlyn Hughes, captain of Liverpool and England, a forceful and exuberant left-half whose charging runs upfield earned him the nickname Crazy Horse, has died aged 57. He underwent surgery for a brain tumour in August last year and his condition deteriorated in the last few days.

In his 12 years at Liverpool Hughes won the League title four times, the European Cup and Uefa Cup twice each, the FA Cup once and the League Cup with his next club, Wolverhampton Wanderers. He won 62 England caps, 23 as captain. After his playing career Hughes became a popular figure on British television, appearing regularly as team captain on the BBC's A Question of Sport. He was also a successful after-dinner speaker.

There is little doubt that his talents were seen to best advantage when he played in midfield, where he could give them the fullest expression. Essentially a right-footed player, he was never wholly at ease when used at left-back. His natural, adventurous instinct was to overlap down the flank but, whenever he did so, however many opponents he left behind, there was always that frustrating moment at the end of the run when he had to switch the ball from his weaker left foot to his powerful right, so that vital seconds were lost and the cross was an inswinger. But he could play in three different positions.

Hughes was born in Barrow, the son of a Welsh international rugby league player who had toured Australia as a forward with the British Lions in 1946. At school he played rugby but soccer appealed to him more and he eventually succumbed to the offers of the manager of Blackpool, Ron Suart. Hughes was then an inside-forward but Blackpool turned him into a left-half and as such he made his debut for them in the 1965-66 season.

The following season he gained a regular place in the side, watched from the terraces by his proud father, who was wont to extol his son's merits to surrounding fans. Hughes played 28 league games that season before Bill Shankly, the famously idiosyncratic manager of Liverpool, a tough Scotsman who had once played right-half for his country, brought him to Anfield for £65,000, then a record sum for a full-back, which at the time he was.

He was fast, he was strong, he tackled well and he showed an enthusiasm which was sometimes branded as excessive. He was boyish to a degree, a quality that would never disappear from his game, and his high voice became familiar to those who could hear it from the field and those who, in later years, saw him on BBC television, not afraid to put his arm around even a princess.

He played 10 First Division games for Liverpool in 1967-68 and thereafter he was an irreplaceable member of a team which grew steadily to dominate not only the English but the European game. He broke into the England team in November 1969, as a left-back in a friendly game against Holland in Amsterdam. When he played against Portugal at Wembley the following December, a game which England unconvincingly won 1-0, one correspondent wrote: 'England's attacking potential was further compromised by the choice of a left-back who won't use his left foot. Emlyn Hughes, a fine, forceful player for Liverpool, ran through often into the empty space on the left. Each time, alas, there was a mandatory hiatus when he carefully adjusted himself to centre with his right foot. This, in an epoch when every second counts, is perfectly absurd and might be distinctly costly were Hughes faced by a better right-winger, Jairzinho [Brazil] or Roger Magnusson [Sweden], who would run him down the line."

Hughes never played in a World Cup. In 1970 he was a member of the England squad which, as holders, competed in Mexico but Alf Ramsey, the manager, preferred the left-footed Terry Cooper and the equally left-footed Bob McNab as cover.

Hughes, however, had a major international career, which lasted to the 1979-80 season when, having joined Wolves from Liverpool, he made his last three appearances for England, two as a substitute.

He was footballer of the year in 1977. With Liverpool he won Championship medals in the 1975-76, 1976-77, 1978-79 and 1979-80 seasons. He appeared for them in three FA Cup finals: losers to Arsenal in 1971, winners against Newcastle United in 1974 and losers against Manchester United in 1977. He played 657 games for Liverpool, scoring 48 goals.

After Arsenal had won the Cup with a late goal by Charlie George, Hughes told Shankly: 'I'm very, very sorry, Boss. That last goal was down to me. I was knackered.' 'That's all right, Emlyn,' Shankly is said to have replied. 'Everybody makes mistakes' – only, as Hughes walked away, to remark unkindly that this was the man who had lost them the Cup final. He was awarded the OBE in 1980.

Two of Hughes' finest achievements were to lead Liverpool to victory in the European Cup finals of 1977 in Rome, against Borussia Mönchengladbach, and at Wembley, in 1978, against Bruges, each time in perhaps his best position, at left-sided centre-back.

After Wolves he played for Rotherham United as player-manager, Hull City, Mansfield Town and Swansea City.

In addition to his TV appearances Hughes worked for Yorkshire-based Real Radio as their main sports pundit for two and a half years. After launching their phone-in, he worked for the station until the end of last season. He was also vice-president of the Dystonia Society, concerned with the neurological disorder. He is survived by his wife, Barbara, son Emlyn and daughter Emma.

Emlyn Hughes, born August 28 1947, died November 9 2004

JULY 1 1996

Dandy defender

BOBBY KEETCH

Bobby Keetch wore a fob watch to make his statement in the 1960s. Professional footballers, only recently freed from the oppressive maximum wage, were moving out of the cap-and-muffler era. And Keetch, who has died of a stroke aged 54, wore that gold watch with pride, tucked into the waistcoat pocket of his blue pinstripe suit.

Today, when millionaire footballers prance in their designer gear, when George Best's non-haircut and romantic exploits are so often recalled, Keetch's clothes may seem staid and bourgeois but then he was consciously defying the stereotype. He did not see why footballers should be categorised as numbskulls, why they should not cultivate their business interests or why they should not have a life outside match day and the training ground. In his own way he was as much a pioneer and trend-setter as Best, though as footballers there was no comparison.

Best was a refulgent star, Keetch a hewer of wood and drawer of water, a centre-half of whom the most benign description might have been uncompromising. 'I could get any labourer off a build-ing site to do what Keetch does,' one of Fulham's reserve defenders was overheard to say in a gym.

There was the sharpest contrast between 'Keetchy' on the field and off it. Blond, squat and muscular, he took no prisoners in the Fulham defence. He was a quick and humorous Londoner – born in Tottenham – like the powerful but erratic outside-left 'Tosh' Chamberlain and he acted as a kind of counterpoint to the artistry of his friend, the immaculate Johnny Haynes, and to the future manager of England, Bobby Robson.

Initially Keetch had joined West Ham United as an apprentice. But his plain methods were hardly suited to the West Ham academy of arts and sciences, while his personality was perfectly attuned to the Fulham of the 1960s, which was the time when football and show business began to overlap.

Those were happy, easy-going days at Fulham – the club he first joined in 1962 – and successful too. On their charming Thames-side ground at Craven Cottage they survived in the First Division. Crowds were large. Celebrities were common both in the stands and on the terraces. Fulham, in fact, was fashionable.

Much was later made of Keetch's affair with an heiress, of his arrival at The Cottage in a Rolls-Royce that was not his own. At the time, however, he talked about it with bewildered modesty. 'Me and little Davie Metchick [Fulham's winger] were driving down the King's Road in the rain when we offer this bird a lift.' The 'bird' accepted and that was how it all began. In the Fulham dressing room before a match, Keetch admitted, with a wry shake of the head: 'I don't know where I am now.'

His confidence grew. Keetch as a character rose high above the mundane Keetch as footballer, which is why he is still remembered in the same sentence as Fulham players who were much more gifted footballers than he was.

His number was up when Vic Buckingham became manager. Buckingham, with his trilby hats and camel-hair coats, had been an unlikely pro footballer; he had passed the educational higher certificate and was a former officer in the RAF. His efforts to turn Keetch into a footballer, rather than a bruiser, were doomed from the start. The little dance Buckingham did on The Cottage turf to encourage Keetch to higher things met with ridicule.

Keetch and his uncompromising methods moved across London to Shepherds Bush and Queens Park Rangers, whom he joined in 1966. Later he played in South Africa with Haynes. But he was always bent on a business career, with many speculations. The last of them, the West End restaurant Football, Football, has only just been launched.

If there were excesses, people readily forgave him. *The Times*'s legendary football correspondent, Geoffrey Green, away on sabbatical, rented Keetch his charming house by the Thames and returned to find it devastated. There were no hard feelings.

One of his best and oldest friends was the comedian Jimmy Tarbuck but 'Keetchy' could span most social categories. As the years went by, he became what that fob watch had suggested. Out of the chrysalis of the clogging footballer came the butterfly of the international entrepreneur.

Bobby Keetch, born October 25 1941, died June 29 1996

DECEMBER 19 2001

Quirk of a keeper's caps

REG MATTHEWS

The goalkeeper Reg Matthews, who has died aged 67, might be said to have lived his career backwards. He won five England caps while with his local club, Coventry City, in the Third Division South, but after joining First Division Chelsea for a then record fee for a goal-keeper of £22,000 he never played for his country again.

Born in Coventry and educated at Barkers Butts school, Matthews joined the club as a 17-year-old in May 1950. He won a regular first-team place in the 1954-55 season, after which his progress was phenomenal. Standing short of 5ft 11in, at just over 12 stone, he was hardly a giant among goalkeepers but his antici-pation, courage and athleticism soon drew the attention of the England selectors. They gave him his first international cap on April 14 1956.

It was a most demanding occasion since the opposition were Scotland at Hampden Park. Matthews did well. A spectacular goal by the little Scottish winger Graham Leggat beat him but Johnny Haynes scored for England and the game finished 1-1. Matthews kept his place for a memorable victory against Brazil at Wembley in May. The Brazilians, still struggling to adapt to a third-back style defence, were penetrated time and again and, although England missed two penalties and Brazil scored twice, England won 4-2.

Matthews now went on England's annual continental tour. In Stockholm he kept a clean sheet against Sweden in a goalless draw. Ten days later, in Berlin, he helped England to a notable 3-1 win against West Germany. His last cap was in October 1956, against Northern Ireland in Belfast, a 1-1 draw. Matthews was then replaced by a far older goalkeeper, the Tottenham veteran Ted Ditchburn.

In the new year, after playing for Coventry more than 100 times, Matthews moved to Chelsea, displacing Bill Robertson and staying for five years, during which he played almost 150 times. By the end of the 1960-61 season he had been displaced there too, by the rising young Peter Bonetti.

The following season he joined Derby County, making more than 200 appearances for them to the end of the 1966-67 season.

He was later player-manager at Rugby and coached Coventry amateurs. From 1968 he worked on the production line at the tractor manufacturer Massey Ferguson. He is survived by his wife, Barbara, a son and a daughter.

Reginald Derrick Matthews, born December 20 1933, died October 7 2001

JANUARY 9 2002

Punter of cool control

CHARLIE MITTEN

Charlie Mitten, who has died aged 80, was the Manchester United winger in Matt Busby's first great side after the Second World War who decamped to Colombia and prospered. His predecessors did not fare so well.

By the time United finished their 1950 summer tour of the United States it seemed that the flight of British players to Bogota had come to an end. It had begun, sensationally, with the clandestine defection of two Stoke City players, Neil Franklin and George Mountford, seduced by the Santa Fe club with an offer of £50 a week, several times the then maximum wage in English football.

It was both a shock and a scandal. Franklin, then the elegant England centre-half expected to play in the imminent World Cup finals in Brazil, had not only ruled himself out of the side but had lied to the Football Association, telling them his withdrawal was because his wife was going to have a baby.

But neither he nor Mountford, an outside-right, found it easy to settle. Nor did the other British players who followed them. All returned with their careers in ruins. Franklin never played for Stoke or England again, sliding down the league to Hull City.

Then, out of the blue, off went Mitten. The move was possible because at that time the Colombians were not members of football's international governing body, Fifa. They had thus been able to attract some of the main Argentinian talents, notably to the Millonarios club. Santa Fe turned, for a time, to English players. In the event Mitten played long enough in Colombia to make plenty of money, after which he calmly came home.

There would be no place for him with Manchester United, his local club and one with which he had been since his teenage years, though he had actually been born in Rangoon. However, after serving a none too onerous suspension, he joined Fulham, with whom, though somewhat heavier than in the past, he played for several impressive seasons. His pace might have been diminished but his renowned balance, cool ball control and notable left foot – adept alike for crosses, shots or penalty kicks – were fully functional.

The war had cut important years out of Mitten's career, though once it was over he established himself as a salient member of the United attack so successfully deployed by Busby, who had just taken over a team without a stadium; Old Trafford had been badly bombed during the war.

The forward line was composed of Jim Delaney, the supposedly brittle-boned Scottish international, Johnny Morris, a quick little inside-right, Jack Rowley, a forceful centre-forward, Stan Pearson and Mitten himself. Mitten, Morris and Pearson were all developed by United.

Altogether Mitten played 161 games and scored 61 goals in his four post-war first-class seasons with United. During those years the club did not win the Championship but were impressive winners of the FA Cup in 1948, beating Blackpool 4-2 in the final after initially falling behind.

Perhaps the most famous match they played in that tournament was at Aston Villa in the third round. Aston Villa scored straight from the kick-off but by half-time United were 5-1 ahead. With nine minutes left Villa had pulled it back to 5-4 but a fine move between Rowley, Delaney and Mitten ended with Keith Jones, in Villa's goal, turning Mitten's drive over the bar and Pearson scoring from the corner.

Mitten, by the time he left United, had played for England once, in an unofficial charity international against Scotland at Maine Road in August 1946. With intense competition for his role he was never to gain a full cap.

In his first season for Fulham in 1951-52, having been amnestied after the South American adventure, he made 16 appearances, scoring half a dozen goals, but could not save them from relegation to the Second Division. The following season he played 40 times for another six goals, forming a notable left-wing pair with the precocious young inside-left, Johnny Haynes. Nine goals in 41 games came in season 1953-54, six in 36 in 1954-55 and four in 21 in 1955-56 but promotion remained elusive.

In 1956 Mitten became manager of Mansfield Town and did well enough there to land a plum post in 1958 at Newcastle United, bringing on Ivor Allchurch, Len White and George Eastham before he was sacked when the club was relegated in 1961. He then became player-manager of non-league Altrincham.

In keeping with his trip to Colombia Mitten was always a betting man. Indeed, it was rumoured that he dealt in horses while in South America. Back in England greyhounds were more his style and he took charge of Manchester's White City stadium in the 1960s, later running a sports promotion business in the city. He was married, with two sons and a daughter.

Charles Mitten, born January 17 1921, died January 2 2002

JULY 29 2004

Half an Ulster force

BERTIE PEACOCK

Bertie Peacock, who has died aged 75 after a heart attack, was a member of the Northern Ireland team that eliminated Italy from the 1958 World Cup and went on to reach the quarter-finals. He was equally important to Celtic, in his dozen years in Glasgow, winning a Championship medal in 1954, Cup medals in 1951 and 1954 and League Cup medals in 1957 and 1958.

Sturdy and compact, Peacock began and ended his career with his local Ulster club, Coleraine. He was an inside-left when he joined Celtic in the 1949-50 season but was converted to left-half. He won the first of his 31 Northern Ireland caps in the 1951-52 season. In 1957-58 he made nine appearances, four of them in the World Cup finals in Sweden, though he was forced to miss the quarter-final against France, which Northern Ireland lost 4-0.

As a wing-half he was the ideal complement to Northern Ireland's right-half, the elegant and inspirational Danny Blanchflower, captain of the team. Peacock was probably a better defensive player and a strong tackler. Having sensationally eliminated the Italians in Belfast from the qualifiers with a 2-1 win, they were badly hit by the loss of Danny's brother, Jackie, a resourceful centre-half, gravely injured in Manchester United's air crash at Munich. But the Czechs were beaten twice, once in the group play-off, the Germans were held to a draw and, though Argentina surprisingly beat the Irish 3-1, later losing 6-1 to Czechoslovakia, Northern Ireland reached the quarter-finals.

Peacock scored 33 goals in his 318 appearances for Celtic, returned to Coleraine in 1961 and the following year became manager of the Northern Ireland team. He then returned to Coleraine for 12 years, during which time he guided the club to its only Irish League title, in 1974. He later managed a public house but sold it in 1990 to concentrate on golf. He is survived by his wife, Ruby, and son, Russell.

Bertie Peacock, born September 29 1928, died July 22 2004

Made by a Sunderland goal

IAN PORTERFIELD

As a football player and manager Ian Porterfield, who has died of colon cancer in a Surrey hospice aged 61, had a plenitude of clubs in a variety of countries, most recently as coach of Armenia, but he will be remembered above all for the sensational goal with which Second Division Sunderland won the 1973 FA Cup final against the powerful favourites, Leeds United.

His goal came after 31 minutes from a Billy Hughes corner. The ball fell to Porterfield, known as a strictly left-footed midfield player, but it was with his right foot that he drove it past the Leeds keeper David Harvey for the only goal of a dramatic game.

Born in Dunfermline, Porterfield was signed by Sunderland from Raith Rovers in December 1967 for what was then the substantial fee of £45,000. In September 1974, omitted by Sunderland from pre-season games, he was granted a transfer but returned to the team before a car crash that December left him with a fractured skull. The injury kept him out until September 1975 and he announced his retirement in August 1976.

Porterfield initially agreed to manage Hartlepool United but changed his mind and decided to go on playing, moving on loan from Sunderland to Reading, then in the Third Division. 'The sole reason I quit,' he explained, 'was because I was sick of hearing about insurance claims and medical reports.' He was at last enabled to leave the north-east for Sheffield Wednesday in July 1977 for £20,000 as player-coach. He had scored 19 goals in 266 appearances for Sunderland.

His first managerial post eventually came in 1979 at Rotherham United, where in 1980-81 he took them up to the Second Division. In July 1981 he moved to Sheffield United, then in the Fourth Division, taking them in three seasons up to the Second while seeing crowds rise to more than 20,000. In March 1986, however, with results by then dismal, he was sacked with five years still on his contract, pocketed £100,000 compensation and the following November was made manager of Aberdeen in succession to Alex Ferguson, who was off to Manchester United after remarkable achievements at Pittodrie. Porterfield later claimed that Ferguson had left behind him a team in decline.

In March 1987 his wife Isa, who married Porterfield when she was 19, left him for a wealthy meat trader. In May 1988, when results were bleak and two weeks after the club directors had given him a vote of confidence, he resigned. Once again he would not be unemployed for long nor would he be long unmarried. In July 1988 he married Elaine Allister – an event marred by a brawl involving his brother Billy and his father, Jack, both of whom were ejected from the reception.

This did not deter Chelsea who, a month later, made him their assistant manager under Bobby Campbell. His methods proved highly popular with the players and he did much to get the club out of the Second Division. But in November 1989 he was off again to manage Reading. That lasted until April 1991, when he was sacked, only to be made full manager of Chelsea two months later.

His demise at Reading coincided with a four-year driving ban for drink-driving, followed in later years by an eight-year ban. He spent £6m on players at Chelsea but few managers lasted long under the impatient and autocratic chairman Ken Bates, who dismissed him in February 1993. Yet again, however, he would not stay out of work for long. When the former Wimbledon and Chelsea striker John Fashanu returned that year from the funeral of the 18 Zambian players who perished in an air crash, he approached Porterfield to take over the national team. This he did successfully but was on the move again in July 1994, signing a vastly lucrative deal to coach a Saudi Arabian club.

That lasted to January 1996, when he returned to England as assistant to Colin Todd, once a team-mate with Sunderland, at Bolton Wanderers. He stayed there only until May, went abroad again to coach the Zimbabwe team but resigned in 1997, citing 'too much unwarranted criticism'.

June 2000 found him coaching Trinidad and Tobago where, in a further instance of bad driving, he ran over and killed a pedestrian. Then in August 2006 he signed a contract to coach the Armenian national team. Though he had been suffering from cancer, he steered Armenia to a surprising 1-1 draw against Portugal last month in a European Championship qualifier in Yerevan.

He had two sons and two daughters with his first wife, two children with his second and is survived by his third wife, Glenda, whom he married in 2002.

John Ian Porterfield, born February 11 1946, died September 11 2007

Steel-back Rovers

Jack Walker

Jack Walker, the Blackburn-born steel magnate, who has died aged 71, stood on the terraces of Blackburn Rovers in the 1950s watching the team's local-born England internationals, Ronnie Clayton and Bryan Douglas, excel, then made a fortune in industry and ploughed much of it back into his beloved football club. Between 1991-92 and 1994-95 he saw the team rise from sustained obscurity to win their first Championship since 1914, only to implode and fall out of the Premier League in 1999, proving perhaps that even in today's football money is not everything.

Walker left school at 14, joined his father's small sheet-metal business, worked variously as sheet-metal worker, welder and a conscript craftsman in the Royal Electrical and Mechanical Engineers and, in 1951, took over the family firm with his brother, Fred.

Together they transformed the business into a steel stockholding concern which, in 1990, Walker sold to British Steel for £360m, before retiring to St Helier, Jersey.

He still, however, commuted regularly to Lancashire for Rovers' games. He had helped them financially in the past but was now able to commit himself fully to the club. Effectively its owner, he remained officially no more than vice-president, although everybody knew who was in command.

Some clue to Walker's determination and entrepreneurial style was given by rhymes and slogans which hung on his office wall. One, the gift of a Blackburn printing company, ran: 'If you think you are out-classed, you are/ You've got to think high to rise/ You've got to be sure of yourself before/ You can ever win a prize/ Life's battles don't always go/ To the stronger or faster man/ But soon or late the man who wins/ Is the fellow who thinks he can.' Another said simply: 'Rule One, I am always right. Rule Two, when I am wrong, read Rule One'.

Despite being estimated the 21st richest man in Britain, the initial transfers Walker funded for Blackburn were relatively unexceptional and, though his signings became more expensive, many were sold on, some at a phenomenal profit. Alan Shearer, the England centre-forward, came from Southampton in July 1992 for £3.3m. Having helped Blackburn win the Championship, he moved on to Newcastle United in July 1996, netting Walker's club £15m in transfer fees.

Signing Shearer was a colossal coup for Walker but persuading Kenny Dalglish to come out of retirement to manage Blackburn was just as important. Dalglish, a renowned Scottish international and manager at Liverpool, had seemingly been devastated by the Hillsborough disaster but went to Ewood Park in 1991.

The following year, after several play-off failures, Blackburn, who had come only sixth in the Second Division, prevailed and entered the inaugural Premier League. Having come fourth in their first season and runners-up in their second, they took the Championship in 1994-95, with Shearer establishing a formidable striking partnership with Chris Sutton, himself bought for £5m from Norwich City and transferred on to Chelsea for double that sum in 1999.

When it came to the European Cup in 1995-96, however, Blackburn went out early, and feebly, to Swedish opposition. The following year Dalglish became general manager and seemed to spend much of his time on the golf course, leaving the managerial job to his coach, Ray Harford, who found it hard to make the transition.

Walker was never tolerant of failure and, in 1997, Harford gave way to Roy Hodgson, who had managed Switzerland and Internazionale, Milan. He, too, failed to bring new success to Blackburn and left in 1998, giving way to the Manchester United coach Brian Kidd. This was another disappointment, so much so that Blackburn, despite frantic expenditure, dropped out of the Premiership in 1999. Kidd did not last out the following season, being replaced by Graeme Souness, like Dalglish a former Liverpool player and manager as well as Scottish international.

Walker was usually a shy and reclusive man, always eager to avoid publicity – except when his team won the Premiership and he exulted on the field. But at the end of 1998-99 he appeared before the fans at rebuilt Ewood Park to exhort them and his players. The ancient stadium had been transformed, a plenitude of back-to-back houses knocked down to accommodate it, not always to the satisfaction of their inhabitants. With a plague of rising damp, the collapse of the cotton industry and a local authority which could not keep pace with such depredations, Blackburn Rovers alone, Jack Walker's creation, assuaged the populace.

He was just as generous in Jersey, where he successfully established his own airline and for many years subsidised and supported the local First Tower United team, happy to sit among the fans to watch their amateur endeavours. 'I get just as much enjoyment from First Tower as I do from watching Rovers,' he said. 'I'm just a dedicated supporter. I've travelled to matches with them on the coach, when the windows have been frozen outside and in. I come to every game and reserve games. I just love it. I even get drunk with them.'

'I was always working,' he used to say. 'Until I got a chauffeur I was driving up to 70,000 miles a year for my various companies and travelling through Europe in the steel industry, mainly to Italy, Belgium and Germany.' By the time he sold his company to British Steel, it was making an annual profit of £48m.

Legends grew up about Walker. In the 1960s, fearful of losing a deal, he is said to have persuaded a taxi-driver to take him through the ravages of Hurricane Donna, more than 1,000 miles down the east coast of America. They arrived, the deal was done and the taxi-driver received an enormous tip.

Colin Jones, the secretary of First Tower for whom Walker bought a training ground, just as he had done for Blackburn, said: 'He's a very down-to-earth man, who loves nothing better than having a drink and a chip butty with the boys after the game. You would never know he had so much money.'

Married to Carol, who survives him with two sons, Walker lived in a huge house amid 30 acres in St Helier. Last May it was announced that he was fighting cancer – news that was all the sadder for the fact that Blackburn, despite his huge expenditure, stayed marooned in the First Division of the Nationwide League.

Jack Walker, born May 19 1929, died August 17 2000

MAY 15 2004

Dennis Wilshaw

GUT-WRENCHING SPIRIT

Dennis Wilshaw, an outstanding attacking footballer with Wolverhampton Wanderers in the 1950s, who has died aged 76 following a heart attack, once remarked of his manager, Stanley Cullis, that team spirit was high 'because we all hated his guts'. Nonetheless, when Cullis was brutally sacked after 16 years, the comment did not prevent the player from sending his old boss a letter of condolence.

Wilshaw was born in Stoke-on-Trent and finished his career with the local club but it was Wolves for whom he first signed in 1944. Qualifying as a schoolmaster, he found himself lent to the then Third Division South club, Walsall, in 1946. In his first season he scored 18 league goals in 35 matches, though this dropped the following season to eight in 36. He established a notable left-wing partnership with the powerful Doug Lishman, who moved on to bigger things with Arsenal.

Essentially left-footed but effortlessly versatile, Wilshaw could play with equal success as outside-left, inside-left or even centre-forward. Wolves recalled him to Molineux early in 1948-49, although it was only late in the season that he was brought into the first team, at centre-forward, scoring 10 goals in 11 games but failing to gain a place in Wolves' FA Cup-winning team. Competition was strong, from Jesse Pye, Jimmy Mullen and Jimmy Dunn. Indeed, the following season he played only eight games, though the previous summer he had gone on tour as centre-forward for the England B team.

Slim but strong, at 5ft 10in and 10st 7lb, Wilshaw was quick and direct, with a powerful shot. Despite his early success at Molineux he did not win a regular place in the attack until 1952-53, scoring 17 goals in 29 games. The following season Wolves won the Championship for the first time. In 39 games Wilshaw scored 25 goals and won his first England cap, against Wales at Cardiff in October 1953. England won 4-1 and he scored twice.

Curiously he did not get another game until the World Cup finals in Switzerland in 1954, when he again demonstrated his opportunism. Omitted from the opening drawn game against Belgium, he played the next against Switzerland in Berne, with Jimmy Mullen outside him on the left wing. Twenty minutes from time, with England 1-0 ahead, Wilshaw took a pass from his right-half Bill McGarry, coolly sold a dummy to three Swiss defenders and scored the second English goal. He kept his place for the quarter-final against Uruguay, in Basle, now deployed at inside-right.

With Stanley Matthews in tremendous form on the right wing, England equalised an early Uruguayan goal when Matthews' shrewdly angled pass allowed Wilshaw to dash through the middle and set up Nat Lofthouse to score. Later Wilshaw flicked the ball just wide when a goal seemed inevitable. England eventually lost 4-2, but with credit.

Altogether Wilshaw won a dozen caps but his most memorable game was that against Scotland at Wembley in April 1955. The Scots were overwhelmed 7-2, four of those goals scored by Wilshaw. That season he had got 20 league goals for Wolves, whose direct, long-passing style was ideally suited to his game.

But in 1955-56, though he scored three times in four games for England, he managed a mere half-dozen goals for Wolves in 25 matches. Season 1957-58 saw him transferred to Stoke City, then in the Second Division, and he was still getting goals for them, 10 altogether, in his final season, 1960-61. Overall he played 378 league games, scoring 172 goals and another 10 for England.

Wilshaw broke his leg in an FA Cup tie in 1961 and, at 35, was forced to retire. He became a senior FA coach, sports psychologist and teacher. His wife, Mary, and daughter, Diane, survive him.

Dennis James Wilshaw, born March 11 1928, died May 10 2004

6

The South Americans

Dead-leaf dinker

DIDI

Waldir Pereira, better known as 'Didi', who has died of pneumonia aged 71, was one of the finest and most influential Brazilian footballers. He represented his country in three World Cups, two of which they won, and survived the humiliation of a *saison en enfer* at Real Madrid immediately after he had played so large a part in Brazil's first ever World Cup victory in 1958. Altogether he played 72 times for Brazil, scoring 24 goals.

Didi was born into an impoverished family in the city of Campos. 'As a kid,' he once said, 'I had to work as a peanut seller to help my parents.' As for so many Brazilian football stars the game was his way out and he never concealed his determination to make as much money as possible. 'A man can speak lightly of poverty only if he has never experienced its terrors,' he said.

His first major club was Fluminense in Rio, whom he joined in 1949. It was there, as an accomplished inside-forward, that he perfected his remarkable dead-leaf free-kicks, struck with the outside of the boot, which swerved and faded their way past any number of baffled goalkeepers.

The most famous of them beat the Peruvians to qualify Brazil for the World Cup finals of 1958, from which Didi was almost excluded. It would have been strange, he wryly reflected afterwards, if they had left out the man who had paid for their ticket. 'From that point,' he wrote much later, 'such kicks became a sort of trademark of mine and everyone asked me, to the point of driving me to desperation, exactly how I did them.'

By then he was an experienced international, having played in the 1954 World Cup in Switzerland, when Brazil were knocked out by Hungary in the quarter-finals in the notorious Battle of Berne. Didi, though, was not one of those who lost his head.

How did he perfect those extraordinary free-kicks? 'Above all,' he wrote, 'a lot of practice and constant practice. For instance, when I joined Botafogo [also of Rio] from Fluminense, in my first period with the club, the Botafogo coach did not care for my long practising with free-kicks and, for a time, the skill was lost to me. The press said, "Such a pity, Didi has forgotten his famous kick." All that happened was that I was not getting the constant practice and this experience taught me how vital this practice was.'

Technically adroit and a superb passer of the ball, Didi fitted admirably into the novel 4-2-4 system practised by Brazil during the 1958 World Cup, playing in Sweden alongside Dino and then the more robustly tackling Zito, though Didi himself was notable for intercepting balls in midfield. He could also score goals from open play, as he had in the 1954 tournament, with goals against Mexico and Yugoslavia in the first round. It was his astonishing, swerving shot from 30 yards out that gave Brazil the lead in the 1958 semi-final in Stockholm and, though he did not score against Sweden in the final, he and Zito dominated the midfield. That other Brazilian legend Pele benefited greatly from Didi's service.

Sadly his 1959-60 interlude with Real Madrid was a disaster because the team's Napoleon, Alfredo di Stéfano, could brook no competition and froze Didi out of the team. Didi later called this 'my so-called failure'. Spanish football, with its physical emphasis, disgusted him. 'Human intelligence and reasoning ability divides us from the animals, so what is a football player who depends solely on his physical strength?'

He went back to Botafogo in Rio and played again for Brazil in the 1962 World Cup in Chile, slower but still influential and disappointed that Di Stéfano did not turn out for Spain when the teams met in Vina del Mar. 'I really wanted to show them the kind of player I was,' he said.

In retirement Didi went to Peru as manager of the Cristal club of Lima, then successfully took over the national team there, qualifying them for the 1970 World Cup at the expense of the ruthless Argentinians and, in Mexico, getting them to the quarter-finals, where they lost honourably to Brazil.

If Madrid 'proved the greatest disillusionment in my life', there would be ample compensations. Between his two stints in Peru Didi returned to Brazil to manage Botafogo, always loyal to the 4-2-4 formation that enabled Peru to beat Argentina away in a vital World Cup qualifier.

Waldir 'Didi' Pereira, born October 8 1929, died May 12 2001

AUGUST 16 2005

Slingshot man

JAIR DA ROSA PINTO

The Brazilian footballer Jair da Rosa Pinto, or Jair as he was always known, who has died from a lung infection aged 84, was part of the dazzling inside-forward trio that seemed sure to win Brazil the World Cup which it staged in 1950. With Zizinho at inside-right and Ademir at centre-forward, the three played football that was a mesmerising amalgam of pace, technique, invention and deadly finishing. Such was the brilliance of Brazil's attack that a leading Italian journalist headlined his article, *Come resistere?* (How to resist?)

Brazil opened the tournament in the huge Maracana Stadium with an easy 4-0 victory over Mexico. Jair scored the second goal, playing, at inside-left and inside-right, either side of the centre-forward, Baltazar. He played no part in the subsequent match, a 2-2 draw against Switzerland in Sao Paulo. Thus it was only in the third game, a hard-fought 2-0 victory over Yugoslavia in Rio, that the trio took the field.

In the first second-round match Brazil met Sweden in Rio and the floodgates opened. In the 19th minute Ademir's speculative shot gave Brazil the lead and he, Zizinho and Jair cut the Swedish defence to pieces. Jair did not score but the trio's combination was of breathtaking intricacy. With Sweden wilting in the heat, they added four goals to their first-half three, running out 7-1 winners. Next came Spain and another half-dozen goals, Jair getting two.

The third, decisive game, in which a draw would be sufficient to make them world champions, came against Uruguay. Fifa had decreed that the tournament's winner – for the first and only time – would be the team that amassed the most points.

Uruguay had already benefited from lopsided organisation, qualifying from the first round after winning a single game 8-0 against feeble Bolivia. But it was largely believed they had no chance against such a brilliant Brazil. The belief was not shared by the Brazilian manager, Flavio Costa, who pointed out that 'the Uruguayan team has always disturbed the slumbers of Brazilian footballers. I'm afraid that my players will take the field on Sunday as though they already had the championship shield sewn on their jerseys.'

At first it seemed that the players' confidence might be justi-fied. Zizinho, Ademir and Jair repeatedly cut through the Uruguayan defence, with Jair, the salient attacker, hitting the post. Two minutes after half-time the Brazilian right-winger Friaca at last gave his team the lead, to tumultuous applause from the

200,000. By the second half, though, Jair was tiring. Juan Schiaffino equalised and Chico Ghiggia scored an astonishing winner.

'I'll take that loss to my grave,' Jair told a Brazilian newspaper. 'And then I'll ask God why we gave away the greatest opportunity to win a World Cup.'

Away from the international scene Jair made the rounds of Brazilian clubs, playing for Flamengo and Vasco da Gama of Rio, Santos, the club which would be made famous by Pele, then the two Sao Paulo clubs, Sao Paulo and Palmeiras.

The Italians categorised Jair as *un fronzoliere* (slingshot man), which could have referred either to his shooting or to the defence-splitting accuracy of his passing. His technique and ball control, as with the other members of the famous trio, were remarkable. Playing for Palmeiras against Nice a year after that catastrophic World Cup in a Sao Paulo tournament, he was eulogised as 'a star, capable of constructing and directing the best attacking actions'. He played until the age of 43. On retiring he managed Santos – where he was said to have nurtured the young Pele – Sao Paulo and Fluminense.

He and his wife, Maria Celia, had two sons.

Jair da Rosa Pinto, born March 21 1921, died July 28 2005

JANUARY 15 2003

Street-wise model

JULINHO

The Brazilian footballer Julinho, who has died after a heart attack aged 73, was an outside-right of tremendous pace, power and skill who scored a spectacular goal against Hungary in the 1954 World Cup in Switzerland. A year later he moved to Florence and played a major role in Fiorentina's first conquest of the Italian Championship. He played 31 of the 34 games, scoring half a dozen goals and creating many more.

He was born in Sao Paulo, though it was with the relatively modest Portuguesa de Desportos that he first emerged. One of six children of a grocery proprietor, he began playing football in the streets and, because of fatherly disapproval, joined the local boys' team, Juvenil Palmeiras. By 16 he was top scorer, with 18 goals, in a team sponsored by the textile union.

Solidly built, Julinho joined the Juventus club of Sao Paulo in 1950 but after six months and for some £25,000 he moved to Portuguesa where, at outside-right, he was an instant success. The following year he toured Europe, scoring seven times. He went on to win medals for the Sao Paulo, Brazilian and South American championships. Most notably he was presented with a gold medal as the only major Brazilian player who, for three seasons, had not been cautioned by a referee.

With a Portuguese father and Italian grandfather it was inevitable that he would draw the attention of European clubs. Internazionale, of Milan, approached him in 1950 but he turned them down following the birth of his son.

He played all three games for Brazil in the 1954 World Cup, scoring in their opening 5-0 win against Mexico, but it was his goal against Hungary in Berne that was truly memorable. Under driving rain in the second half, as violence raged, Hungary were leading when Julinho, in the words of one observer, 'after a magnificent swirling dribble at fantastic speed, shot a thunderbolt past [Gyula] Grosics to make it 2-3'. The Hungarians eventually won 4-2 and Brazil were out. By the 1958 World Cup Julinho was in Italy and not chosen. In all he played 31 games for his country, scoring 13 goals.

He returned to Brazil in 1959 and was promptly picked to play against England in Rio. This was bad luck for Blackpool's Jimmy Armfield, who was whimsically awarded his first cap at left-back – on his wrong foot. Julinho ran him ragged, scoring the first Brazilian goal in a 2-0 victory. On the field he cut a withdrawn, implacable, almost statuesque figure.

Julinho (Julio Botelho), born August 5 1929, died January 11 2003

JANUARY 27 2004

Black Diamond

LEONIDAS DA SILVA

The Brazilian footballer Leonidas da Silva, known as the 'Black Diamond', who has died aged 90 after long years of Alzheimer's disease and diabetes, was master of the bicycle kick, which brought him many of his goals. He scored eight in the World Cup finals of 1938 in France, though he did not win a medal because he was left out of the team that lost to Italy in the semi-finals in Marseille.

Leonidas was the more phenomenal for being so small a centre-forward, though he began as an inside-right. Of him it was said by football historian Jerry Weinstein: 'He was as fast as a greyhound, as agile as a cat and seemed not to be made of flesh and bones at all but entirely of rubber. He was tireless in pursuit of the ball, fearless and constantly on the move. He never conceded defeat. He shot from any angle and any position and compensated for his small height with exceptionally supple, unbelievable contortions and impossible acrobatics.'

In Brazil he had a second nickname, the Magia Negra or black magician. He made his name as a teenage inside-right with the Bonsucesso club of Rio de Janeiro in 1931. When Rio played Sao Paulo in the Brazilian championship play-off he was picked, scored twice in a 3-0 win and was promptly chosen for the Brazilian squad to meet Uruguay in the annual Rio Branco tournament.

He was then a reserve but the following year he was a first choice in the same competition and scored both Brazilian goals when Uruguay were beaten 2-1 in Montevideo, a feat that led to his being signed, in 1933, by Peñarol, one of Uruguay's two dominant clubs. The following year saw him back in Brazil, helping to win the championship. He was then chosen for the 1934 World Cup squad, though his team lasted a single game, against Spain, in a knock-out tournament. Leonidas led the attack but had inadequate support in a team of gifted individuals which lacked coherence. His inside-forwards were sparkling ball players but tended, especially in the second half, it was said, 'to show their party tricks'. Brazil lost 3-1.

Curiously at the time of the 1938 World Cup Leonidas was not the leading scorer in Brazilian football. That distinction belonged to 'King' Niginho, who went to France but never played. Leonidas, in the meantime, had joined another famous Rio club, Botafogo, in 1935 and, a year later, yet another, Flamengo. When he arrived in France he had already won 30 international caps.

A remarkable first-round match against Poland saw Brazil win 6-5. Two first-half goals by Leonidas, undeterred by the muddy conditions, saw Brazil 3-1 ahead at half-time. At one point in the second half he took off his boots and threw them across the touch line to his trainer, Pimenta, but the Swedish referee made him put them on again. An extraordinary rally by the Poles saw them level at 4-4 but Leonidas completed his hat-trick in extra-time and Brazil ran out winners by the odd goal of 11. Leonidas was only the second highest scorer in the match, Ernst Willimowski creating World Cup history with four.

Next came Czechoslovakia in Bordeaux, a 1-1 draw, with Leonidas scoring for Brazil in a brutal affair in which he himself limped off the field. Two days later Brazil, with nine changes, won a perfectly calm replay on the same ground 2-1, Leonidas in coruscating form getting his country's first goal. Excluded from the semi-final, he gained some consolation with two goals in the third-place match, won 4-2 against Sweden, to finish top scorer for the tournament with seven.

In 1941 Leonidas was jailed for eight months for forging a certificate exempting him from army service. After six years at Flamengo, and out of prison, he joined Sao Paulo in 1942, scoring 14 goals for a Championship medal. He briefly worked as a coach with Sao Paulo and as a private detective. For the next 20 years he was a radio commentator.

Leonidas da Silva, born September 6 1913, died January 24 2004

25 FEBRUARY 2004

Stopper for starters

ROQUE MASPOLI

In July 1950 the stupendous goalkeeping of Roque Maspoli, who has died aged 86, enabled Uruguay to beat the favourites Brazil and win the World Cup in the Maracana stadium, Rio, in front of 200,000 astonished spectators. Forty-seven years later, at the age of 79, he was put in charge of his country's waning international team, an extraordinary tribute to an icon of the Uruguayan game.

He began as a full-back, made his name as a goalkeeper with one of Uruguay's two main clubs, Nacional of Montevideo, later switched to the other, Peñarol, and went on to manage both.

Maspoli was essentially a shot stopper – brave, flexible and immensely agile, with superb anticipation. Like so many continental and South American keepers he was less effective at dealing with high centres from the wings.

But that performance against Brazil could scarcely have been surpassed. He had played in the initial 8-0 walkover against Bolivia, the only time Uruguay had to play in the preliminary phase. He let in two goals in the final pool, when Uruguay drew 2-2 with Spain, but missed the match against Sweden, which was won 3-2. Such form did nothing to suggest they could contain Brazil, who had scored 13 goals in their two final pool games, against the same opposition as the Uruguayans.

Euphoria was widespread among Brazilian fans. Scarcely anyone heeded the words of Flavio Costa, Brazil's manager: 'The Uruguayan team has always disturbed the slumbers of Brazilian footballers. I'm afraid that my players will take the field on Sunday as though they already had the championship shield sewn on their jerseys. It isn't an exhibition game. It is a match like any other, only harder.'

And so it proved. In the early stages Brazil's dazzling attack, composed of Zizinho, Ademir and Jair, overwhelmed Uruguay's defence. Maspoli made two great saves and gradually Uruguay's attack came into the game, though in the last few minutes of the first half it was Maspoli alone who prevented a Brazilian goal.

A couple of minutes into the second half Ademir and Zizinho skilfully drew the Uruguayan defence towards the left. The consequent cross found Friaca racing in from the right to take the ball in his stride and put Brazil ahead. But after 20 minutes Juan Schiaffino stunned the crowd by equalising for Uruguay. Much of the steam seemed to go out of the Brazilians and, 11 minutes from the end, Chico Ghiggia, the outside-right who had set up Schiaffino's goal, shot the winner.

Uruguay took a powerful squad to Switzerland for the 1954 World Cup finals. Maspoli did not let in a goal in the two opening pool games, won 2-0 against the Czechs and 7-0 against the Scots, though England, in the quarter-finals, were a harder proposition. This time Maspoli was beaten twice, by Nat Lofthouse and Tom Finney, but the erratic goalkeeping of his opposite number, Gil Merrick, condemned England to a 4-2 defeat and took Uruguay into the semi-finals.

Maspoli had put on weight and tended to punch away crosses rather than catch them. This proved fatal in the course of a wonderful semi-final against Hungary, when Sandor 'Golden Head' Kocsis headed a couple of late goals to put Uruguay out of the reckoning, 4-2. In the third-place match against Austria Uruguay's disenchanted team lost 3-1.

Retiring as a player, Maspoli became the successful manager of his old club, Peñarol. In 1966 he took them to the final of the Libertadores Cup, the South American club championship, in which they beat River Plate of Buenos Aires. This qualified them to meet Real Madrid, the formidable European Cup holders, for the so-called Intercontinental Championship. In Montevideo Peñarol won 2-0 but few expected them to hold out in the return game in Madrid. Instead they recorded another 2-0 win and thus became world club champions.

In the 1980s Maspoli spent several years coaching the Uruguay team, before being recalled as national manager in 1997. He is survived by his wife, Irene Estramil, and their daughter, Irene.

Roque Gaston Maspoli, born October 12 1917, died February 22 2004

OCTOBER 1 2002

Crazy Legs

JULIO PEREZ

There were 12 minutes left in the astonishing last match of the 1950 World Cup, at the Maracana stadium in Rio de Janeiro. Though decisive and dramatic, it was not the final. Instead a ludicrously prolix system decreed that the winners on points of the final four teams would take the trophy. This meant that a draw with Uruguay would give victory to the dazzling Brazilian hosts.

Their scintillating inside-forward trio of Zizinho, Ademir and Jair had besieged the gallant Uruguayan defence, which had fallen behind just after half-time to a goal by the right-winger, Friaca. Yet Uruguay's Juan Schiaffino had equalised and now their inside-right, Julio Perez, took a pass from his fragile but dynamic right-winger, Chico Ghiggia.

He was challenged strongly but dashed on to touch the ball back to Ghiggia, who drove it past the Brazilian keeper, Moacir Barbosa. No player had done more to engineer his team's 2-1 success than Perez, who has died in Montevideo, aged 76.

Like Ghiggia and Schiaffino, Perez's promotion to his national team had been fortuitous. In 1949, faced with a strike by its professional players, Uruguay, rather than withdraw from the South American championships, sent a team of amateurs, including those three. Their side was trounced 5-1 by the Brazilian hosts but within the year they had established themselves as regular members of the side which, earlier in 1950, returned to Brazil to contest the Rio Branco Cup. This consisted of three matches and, encouragingly for Uruguay, there was little between their team and Brazil. Uruguay won 4-3 in Sao Paulo but lost 3-2 and 1-0 in Rio. When it came to the World Cup they had the good fortune to be in a group of two, the other being feeble Bolivia. They won 8-0, though Perez did not score.

Renowned as an inside-left with his club, Nacional of Montevideo, he felt obliged, given the luminous form of Schiaffino, to operate at inside-right but he was just as effective there – a splendid ball player, quick to make the telling pass and no mean finisher. When Uruguay entered the final pool, and met Spain in Sao Paulo, he played an outstanding part in the 2-2 draw. Next came a hard-fought victory over Sweden, probably Perez's best and most influential match of the tournament. 'There is no doubt,' it was reported, 'that Perez, more than anyone else, turned the game for Uruguay.'

The decider against Brazil was played in front of 200,000 people and the longer the game went on, the more dangerous Perez became. Two minutes into the second half Friaca got his goal and a cacophonous public celebrated what seemed an inevitable home victory. But a few minutes later Perez inspired his side with two shots that showed what was possible. Barbosa stopped the first without great trouble but, when Perez, receiving from Schiaffino, dashed through a gap in the Brazilian defence, his fulminating right-footed shot was reached desperately by Barbosa with the tips of his fingers. It was a magnificent save, sadly forgotten when Brazil's first black goalkeeper was blamed for his team's defeat.

Born in Montevideo, Perez first emerged as a footballer in Buenos Aires, Nacional bringing him home in 1950. He continued with them until 1957, helping to win four championships, and retired in 1963, going on to coach youth teams for 23 years in Uruguay, Paraguay and Mexico. His nickname of 'Crazy Legs' was a tribute to his ball play.

Julio Gervasio Perez Gutierrez, born June 19 1926, died September 21 2002

Maracana silenced

JUAN SCHIAFFINO

Despite being pale and slender and looking the antithesis of the footballer as athlete, the Uruguayan Juan Alberto Schiaffino, who has died aged 77, was one of the great inside-forwards of his day. He had exquisite ball control, a gimlet eye for the telling pass and a left foot that scored many an important goal.

Unquestionably the most important was his equaliser against Brazil in the decisive game of the 1950 World Cup. It shocked into silence the 200,000-strong crowd in the new Maracana stadium and spurred Uruguay to go on and lift the cup, winning 2-1.

Four years later Tommy Docherty, the hard-tackling wing-half who marked Schiaffino when Uruguay thrashed Scotland 7-0 in the 1954 World Cup in Basle, called him the greatest player he had ever faced. Docherty talked of the moment when he felt he had Schiaffino penned in on the goal-line, only to find the Uruguayan, almost magically, slipping past him.

Born in Montevideo, Schiaffino made his mark with Peñarol, one of that city's two famous clubs. A players' strike before the 1949 South American Cup tournament meant the Uruguayans entered a team made up, technically, of amateurs but, as one of them, Schiaffino comfortably held his own against more established players. By 1950 he was a major star, an outstanding positional player who could dribble past opponents with ease.

The vagaries of the 1950 competition, which attracted only 13 finalists, meant that, to qualify for the final pool, Uruguay had merely to beat the feeble Bolivians. This they did 8-0, with

Schiaffino helping himself to four goals. A contorted system decreed there be no final as such but the winners of a final pool would take the cup. Brazil, with a one-point lead over Uruguay, needed only a draw in the last game to be champions.

Uruguay held out against terrific pressure, with Brazil urged on by a fanatical crowd. When Friaca scored for Brazil early in the second half, that seemed to be that – except that in the first half Schiaffino had twice threatened a goal. When served by Oscar Miguez, and the little right-winger Chico Ghiggia, he struck a shot which the Brazilian keeper, Moacir Barbosa, only just managed to reach. Then, coming suddenly to life from seeming torpor, Schiaffino dribbled his way clean through Brazil's defence, only for Barbosa to frustrate him again.

For all the crowd's triumphalism, the warning was there. Schiaffino had plainly found the range. In the second half Uruguay counter-attacked often and crisply. Obdulio Varela, their heroic centre-half and captain, sent Ghiggia flying down the right wing. His cross, astoundingly, found Schiaffino unmarked. He took four strides forward, then walloped his shot past Barbosa. Fourteen minutes later Ghiggia scored the winner.

The rich Italian clubs made strenuous efforts to buy Schiaffino, particularly in 1951. Roma offered half a million pesos and Juventus sent their Fiat patron, Gianni Agnelli, to Montevideo. Schiaffino was keen to go to the land of his ancestors but Peñarol would not let him. There were rumours that the player had his passport ready to take off for Colombia, then outside the international body, Fifa. In the event he stayed and, though Uruguay did not retain their World Cup in Switzerland in 1954, he and they gave a fine account of themselves.

In their opening game Schiaffino scored the second goal in a 2-0 win against Austria. Then came the demolition of Scotland. Although he did not score, Schiaffino pulled the strings throughout, showing an almost clairvoyant understanding with his centre-forward Miguez. Next, in a sweltering quarter-final, England gave Uruguay a powerful run for their money. But it was Schiaffino's controversial goal to make it 3-1 that tipped the balance, benefiting from Varela's illicitly taken free-kick. When injuries led Uruguay to realign their forces Schiaffino, in the words of a commentator, 'was withdrawn to take over the central defensive position, from where he was to show his real mastery as one of the greatest and most balanced all-round footballers on the contemporary scene'.

In a magnificent semi-final against Hungary a depleted Uruguayan team virtually used Schiaffino as centre-forward. With 15 minutes left and Uruguay 2-0 down, his pass sent Juan Hohberg, a naturalised Argentinian, racing through to score. Three minutes from time Schiaffino made Hohberg the equaliser but Hungary scored twice in extra-time. In the meaningless third-place match against Austria Schiaffino yet again sent Hohberg clear to score the first goal, though weary Uruguay lost the game 3-1.

Now Italy really beckoned. For a record fee of £72,000, pocketing £23,000 himself, Schiaffino joined AC Milan, fitting in at once and helping his new team to win the Championship; he played in all but seven games. Less than six months after his last game for Uruguay he was playing for the Italians against Argentina.

This was a shameless exploitation of his double nationality but an all too familiar one. Three years later he was capped by Italy again, in their ill-starred game against Northern Ireland at Belfast, a match meant to be a World Cup eliminator but played as a so-called friendly because the Hungarian referee was held up by fog. With a ferocious kick that broke Wilbur Cush's shin-pad and could have broken his leg Schiaffino showed a less pleasing side of his character.

In 1955-56 he helped Milan to reach the semi-finals of the first European Cup, which they lost to Real Madrid, won another Championship medal in 1957 and played a salient role in the 1958 European Cup final, when Real again just beat Milan. Used at centre-forward, Schiaffino scored Milan's first goal from a pass by Nils Liedholm, though, unlike Liedholm, he did not go on to the 1958 World Cup finals. He won his last two Italian caps in the eliminators against Portugal and Northern Ireland.

In 1960 Schiaffino was transferred to Roma, where he played only in carefully chosen games. Two years later he returned to Uruguay, becoming first a scout, then manager of his old club, Peñarol, and of the national team. His shrewd business dealings had already guaranteed him a comfortable future.

Juan Alberto Schiaffino, born July 28 1925, died November 13 2002

APRIL 5 2002

Free scorer, free spirit

VAVA

Edvaldo Isidio 'Vava' Neto, who has died of heart trouble aged 67, was Brazil's dynamic, goal-scoring centre-forward in the 1958 World Cup final in Sweden and in 1962 in Chile. In Stockholm, after Brazil had fallen behind to an early Swedish goal, Vava swept the ball in twice, to change the game, after a couple of devastating runs down the right and passes pulled back into the middle by the right-winger Garrincha. In the final in Santiago he scored Brazil's third goal when the Brazilian right-back Djalma Santos looped a ball high into the sun and the hapless Czech keeper, Viliam Schroiff, dropped it.

Vava was always good for goals, whether they were gifts or snatched through brisk opportunism. In 1962's quarter-final against England in Vina del Mar he swooped after Garrincha's long-range free-kick bounced off the chest of the England goalkeeper, Ron Springett. And he headed two goals in Brazil's semi-final victory against Chile.

Born in Recife, he first played for the local club. In 1951 he began a seven-year spell with Rio's Vasco da Gama, leaving after the 1958 World Cup final, his 17th international game, to try his luck for three years with Atlético Madrid. Back in Sao Paulo he joined Palmeiras and forced his way into the World Cup team and the attack in Chile.

Vava was a strong, brave, thrustful player with excellent technique. When the 1958 series started, the preferred centre-forward was the 19-year-old Mazzola (Jose Altafini) but Brazil's manager, Vicente Feola, felt his head had been turned by a lucrative transfer to Milan, so Vava came in for the third game, in Gothenburg, scoring twice against Russia.

He first tasted international football as an amateur at the 1952 Olympics in Helsinki. In Recife, however, he was forced to move on by the local club's dependence on more experienced men. So before winning a first-team place he played for Vasco in Rio, initially as a wing-half.

Vava greatly enjoyed his years in Madrid but preferred the flexibility of Brazilian coaches. 'They have their theories but they do not entrap their players with them. They recognise an established player is a man of accomplishment, fond of the game and having the ability to change the course of a battle by his own initiative when necessary.'

He went on to Mexico and the United States but concluded the

1960s with Portuguesa in Rio, before going into management in Brazil, Mexico and Spain. In the 1982 World Cup he was assistant coach. He also ran the Qatar national side. He was married with four children.

Edvaldo Isidio 'Vava' Neto, born November 12 1934, died January 19 2002

7

Made in Europe

Corruptor's art

ITALO ALLODI

The career of the football impresario and art collector Italo Allodi, who has died aged 71, may be seen almost as a paradigm of Italian public life in the 1960s and after. The son of a railwayman, he was born in Asagio and rose from journeyman professional footballer to become rich and respected. Long after he had been pilloried as a corruptor of referees he dominated the football transfer market, possessed a fine art collection and was appointed by the Italian Football Federation to important roles.

'*Non è un corrotto, è un corruttore* [he's not corrupt, he's a corruptor],' said Gian Paolo Ormezzano, a leading Turin journalist. It was sometimes difficult to tell the difference but, for all the obloquy that was piled on Allodi at times, Italy's football press continued to beat a reverential path to his door.

After his death Italian papers eulogised him as a positive influence on their football, ignoring his feud with Enzo Bearzot, manager of Italy's 1982 World Cup-winning team, and his involvement in the scandals of the 1960s and 1970s, when referees of European Cup games were bribed by his clubs Inter, then Juventus.

Allodi emerged initially at Mantua, with the Mantova football club, which in the middle and later 1950s made an extraordinary rise from the depths of the Italian fourth division to reach Serie A in the 60s. As the club's secretary he attracted the attention of the powerful Milanese club Internazionale and became its secretary and main wheeler-dealer in the early 1960s.

This would be the time of the club's greatest triumphs and of its most doubtful activities. Its owner and patron was the oil magnate Angelo Moratti, who poured fortunes into the club but believed, in football parlance, in getting his retaliation in first – not least when it came to matches in the European Cup and the suborning of referees. The team's manager was the flamboyant, volatile and sometimes ruthless Helenio Herrera, an Argentinian brought up in Casablanca. Dezso Solti, a Hungarian refugee, held no official position with the club but was responsible for seducing referees; and he answered directly to Allodi.

Three successive return legs of European Cup semi-finals were involved. In 1964 a Yugoslav referee Branko Tesanic, who had failed to send off an Inter player for kicking an opponent, was reported to be on an Adriatic holiday at Inter's expense. In 1965 Liverpool were so badly cheated by the refereeing of a Spaniard, Ortiz de Mendibil, that their half-back Tommy Smith kicked him all the way to the dressing room. In 1966 a brave Hungarian referee was spirited up to Moratti's villa and offered, in the presence of Allodi and Solti, numerous gifts. After refusing to bend the game against Real Madrid he never got another European match.

In 1974 Juventus, where Allodi had become general manager, were accused with Solti and Allodi of trying to bribe an honest Portuguese referee, Fernando Marques Lobo, to fix a 1973 European Cup semi-final against Derby County. Allodi maintained his innocence but Uefa, the European body which in 1973 had exonerated Juventus after a farcical disciplinary hearing in Zurich, did suspend Solti *sine die*.

In 1974, to widespread surprise, Allodi was made general manager of the Italian World Cup team in West Germany, although his mandate was seen as a disaster. Italy, accused of trying to bribe the Poles who eliminated them, fared dismally.

The following year Allodi was asked to draw up a plan for the national coaching centre at Coverciano, outside Florence. Once again he seemed scarcely qualified for the task but he finished up in charge of the place, where he implemented an expensive 'super course' for coaches, which entailed sending them abroad. Fulvio Bernardini, a former Italian international and manager of the national team, expressed his amazement. 'All Allodi knows how to do,' he said, 'is give gold watches to referees.'

Allodi was still in charge at Coverciano when Bearzot took the Italian team to the World Cup finals in Spain. It began badly. At a conference in Coverciano a young Tuscan manager, Eugenio Fascetti, known to be a protégé of Allodi, made a vicious attack on Bearzot, claiming that he was traducing the whole of Italian football. 'How can I function,' demanded Bearzot, 'when I have a Brutus at my back?' 'If I'm Brutus,' responded Allodi, 'he must think he is Caesar.' Bearzot had the last laugh, though. Italy won the World Cup.

In 1982, after that World Cup success, Allodi left Coverciano to become general manager of Fiorentina but did not get on with the owners, the Pontello family. In 1985 he took a similar post at Napoli, who won their first ever Italian Championship during his five-year spell. It was ironic that when, eventually and tearfully, Allodi appeared before a football tribunal in Naples he turned out to be innocent of the charges.

Times slowly changed. Allodi continued to give generous presents, especially to journalists. But when Lino Cascioli, of the Roman daily *Il Messagero*, received a painting, he sent back one of the same value.

Allodi leaves a widow, Franca, and a son, Cristiano.

Italo Allodi, born April 13 1928, died June 3 1999

AUGUST 16 2003

Emma's moment

LOTHAR EMMERICH

The tall, strongly built outside-left Lothar 'Emma' Emmerich, who has died of cancer aged 61, had a short but significant international career for the West German national side. He played a major role in his team's contentious last-minute equaliser against England at Wembley in the World Cup final of July 1966.

Hitherto the only thing of note that Emmerich had done in that game, which was not one of his best, was to force a save in the first half from Gordon Banks. The England goalkeeper had blocked a shot from Wolfgang Overath and the ball ran to Emmerich. He struck it well but too straight and Banks held the shot.

But in the 90th minute of normal time, with England 2-1 ahead and seeming to have the cup won, West Germany were awarded a questionable free-kick just outside the England penalty area. Jack Charlton, the centre-half, was penalised for a foul on Siggi Held, though it looked as if the striker had backed into Charlton. At all events Emmerich, who had a formidable left foot, took the kick to the left of the goal and drove it into the goalmouth. There it struck the German defender Karl-Heinz Schnellinger in the back, causing him to put both his hands behind him when he felt the pain and creating a *trompe l'oeil*, which made it look as if he had handled the ball. He had not and it found its way to the far post, where Wolfgang Weber drove home the equaliser.

So the game went into extra-time and England went ahead with a still more controversial goal when Geoff Hurst's shot hit the underside of the bar from which the ball bounced down and may or may not have crossed the line. This time the ruling favoured England, who went on to win 4-2.

Emmerich, who scored 115 goals in 183 games for Borussia Dortmund, was a very late choice for the West German team. He made his debut in Rotterdam on March 23 1966, scoring one of the goals in his team's 4-2 victory. Picked for the World Cup squad, he was not chosen for the first two games, against Switzerland and Argentina, but came into the third game of the qualifying group, against Spain at Villa Park. There he hit one of the most spectacular goals of the competition – Germany's first in a 2-1 win – with a long-range shot of tremendous power.

He retained his place for the Germans' subsequent three matches – the ill-tempered quarter-final against Uruguay at Hillsborough, won 4-0, the semi-final against the USSR at Everton, won 2-1, and the final itself. And that concluded his international career: five caps, two goals.

For Borussia Dortmund, between 1963 and 1969, Emmerich figured in the team that won the West German Cup in 1965 and, shortly before the World Cup finals, won the European Cup-Winners' Cup, beating Liverpool in Glasgow. He later became the fan coordinator for Dortmund.

Lothar Emmerich, born November 29 1941, died August 14 2003

November 13 2004

Valiant Alsatian

OSCAR HEISSERER

Oscar Heisserer, captain of France's national football team who has died aged 90, was the Alsatian inside-forward who, nobly and bravely, held out against wartime German pressure first to join the SS, then to play for Germany.

Heisserer was born in Strasbourg, the capital of Alsace, which had been French until the Franco-Prussian war in 1870 and French again from 1919 until the fall of France in 1940. Slender, pallid and blond in his prime, he looked a great deal more German than French but it was emphatically as a Frenchman that he saw himself. Racing Strasbourg was his club, to which he cleaved with exemplary loyalty under the greatest Nazi pressure.

His international career, spanning 11 years and 23 caps, would certainly have been more extensive had it not been for the Second World War. It began on October 31 1937, some months after he had played inside-left for Racing Strasbourg in the French Cup final when they lost 2-1 to Sochaux at the Stade Colombes in Paris. He was at inside-left that day but at inside-right when France beat Holland 3-2 in Amsterdam.

Either inside-forward position was acceptable to him; he was a gifted player, a shrewd passer of the ball, who could score important goals – notably the 89th-minute equaliser at Wembley in May 1945 which unexpectedly gave France, scarcely recovered from the war, a 2-2 draw against England.

He had been enlisted in the French army and in 1940 was fighting on the Maginot Line. He had returned to his native Strasbourg and one day was about to leave the Racing Club ground when three cars drove up, disgorging SS soldiers. Heisserer was taken to SS headquarters where the local commandant told him that since Strasbourg would now be German, he had better join the SS. Heisserer's bold reply was to the effect that the previous day he had been the captain of France, 'so how can I join the SS today?' After a three-hour grilling he was freed, though told he would regret his decision.

Heisserer kept his place in the French team after his debut and appeared in their two matches when France staged the 1938 World Cup final. He was at inside-right when Belgium were beaten 3-1 in the first round and again, in the second round, when Italy eliminated France 3-1, though Heisserer scored the French goal.

Sepp Herberger, Germany's formidable manager, came all the way to Strasbourg during the war to try to persuade Heisserer to play for the Germans but Heisserer stoutly refused. Instead his international career, crowned with the captaincy of France, lasted until 1948.

When he retired he became in 1951 the first manager of the newly formed Olympique Lyonnais and later of his local team, Strasbourg. He returned to banking and then ran a shoe-making company.

Oscar Heisserer, born July 18 1914, died October 6 2004

NOVEMBER 11 1997

Tyrant magician

HELENIO HERRERA

The remarkable and authoritarian football manager Helenio Herrera, who has died aged 81, once observed that his whole career had been a triumph. He believed it.

Born of Argentinian parents, brought up in Casablanca's slums and brought to France, where he was naturalised, in 1934, he became a professional footballer. A competent, unexceptional defender, he played for Red Star of Paris, Charleville, Stade Français and Roubaix but never won a full French cap.

It was as a manager, though, that he made his mark, in France, Spain and finally in Italy. He managed all three countries' national teams but it was Spain he took to the 1962 World Cup finals in Chile, though with limited success.

A flamboyant figure, with a brooding presence, Herrera first managed the two Parisian teams for whom he had played: Red Star and Stade Français. He then took over at Valladolid in Spain but established his credentials at Atlético Madrid, with whom he won the Spanish Championship in 1950 and 1951. Spells at Sevilla, La Coruña and Malaga followed but it was with Barcelona that he forged a European reputation. He built a team that included three Hungarians, the veteran Ladislao Kubala, Zoltan Czibor and Sandor Kocsis, Evaristo of Brazil, Eulogio Martínez of Paraguay and the creative Spanish inside-forward Luis Suarez who would follow him to Internazionale of Milan.

Il Mago (the magician), as he came to be known, imposed his rituals on the Barcelona team, above all in the European Cup. In a vast, bare room he would put them through exhausting exercises. These done, he would throw a football at each of them in turn, first to head, then to foot, the player being expected to pounce on it like a predator. 'A sort of fury seemed to possess the players,' wrote an observer.

The players then took showers, returned and formed a circle with Herrera at its centre, throwing a ball to each in turn, shouting questions like 'What do you think of the match? Why are we going to win? How are we going to play?'

Evaristo would respond, 'We'll win because we want to win.' Antonio Ramallets, the Spanish international goalkeeper, rejoined: 'We're one of the best teams in the world; that's why we'll win.' But Kubala, who had seen it all and played for Czechoslovakia, Hungary and Spain itself, stood by in silence. His days were numbered.

Wolves, then England's best team, were thrashed in the mud of Molineux by a Barcelona team which made light of conditions that should have suited Wolves' long-ball, somewhat basic style. Barcelona won 5-2. But in 1960, and the semi-finals, Barcelona and Herrera met their Waterloo or rather their Real Madrid. Things might have been different had the manager included Kubala and Czibor but they had quarrelled with him over bonuses and, to the displeasure of the Barcelona fans, they were passed over. Barcelona were beaten, home and away, and angry fans attacked Herrera in the street. He was sacked.

Now he left Spain for Italy and Milan, where he became manager of Internazionale. Its millionaire president, Angelo Moratti, known as Il Gran Petrolifero, the great oil man, was deeply ambitious and none too finicky about how Inter attained their objectives. Referees were regularly approached.

Herrera decided that creative, attacking football put too much at risk. He embraced *catenaccio*, sweeper defence, with which Inter had won the Italian league almost a decade earlier. His Livornese sweeper, Armando Picchi, seldom strayed beyond the halfway line. Suarez was bought to control the midfield. Tall Giacinto Facchetti was the attacking left-back who often scored goals. Sandrino Mazzola was an elegant forward. But the team and its parsimonious methods made few friends.

Gerry Hitchens, an England 1962 World Cup player who had entered the professional game through a welfare miners' team in Shropshire, described Herrera's methods as oppressive. It was 'like coming out of the army,' he said after he had left the club. Herrera would pin up notices in the dressing room: 'Attack: More Than 100 Goals! Defence: Less Than 30 Goals!' The players were constantly being sent into ritiro, training camp, before games. Hitchens was particularly put out by the way, when the coach took off for the local airport after an away game, Herrera would yell: 'Pensa alla partita' (Think about the next game).

The medicine worked. Inter won the 1963, 1965 and 1966 Italian Championships, the European Cup (which had eluded him at Barcelona) in 1964 and 1965 and the Intercontinental Cup in both these years.

By 1967 the team was fading and lost 2-1 to Celtic in the European final in Lisbon. Bill Shankly, Liverpool's idiosyncratic Scots manager, who was at the post-game banquet, said he detailed two Celtic coaches to abuse Herrera for his methods, which Shankly, knowing Liverpool had been cheated by Inter in the 1965 semi-final, despised.

The following year Herrera became Roma's manager on what was then a stupendous £90,000 contract. Things were harder in that Byzantine milieu, though he did take the team to the semifinals of the European Cup-Winners' Cup in 1970, where they lost to Gornik Zabrze on the toss of a coin. With Roma he continued to be his bombastic self, sneering that the only time Roma had won the Championship, in 1941, it was because 'Mussolini was the manager'.

Herrera could be quite a dictator himself. Once, falling behind on a training run at Inter's training ground, Hitchens, Suarez and the left-winger, Marioliro Corso, saw the team coach drive off without them, leaving them to cover six miles back to base.

More serious was the case of Roma's talented forward, Giuliano Taccola who had been ill for some time. A tonsillectomy was of no avail. Roma's doctors warned that Taccola had a heart murmur, the result of a congenital defect. But Herrera insisted there was nothing wrong with him. In March 1969, when Roma were playing Cagliari in Sardinia, Taccola had travelled with the team, though he was not to play. The manager insisted that he train in the morning with the rest of the squad on a beach buffeted by icy winds. Taccola developed a high fever, watched the game from the stand, collapsed afterwards in the dressing room and died.

Herrera never did win the championship with Roma, though so popular was he that his salary was quickly covered by season-ticket sales. On retirement he went to live in Venice, continuing to fulminate against those he considered his inferior successors in the game.

Helenio Herrera, born April 17 1916, died November 9 1997

FEBRUARY 20 2002

Deep-lying demon

NANDOR HIDEGKUTI

Nandor Hidegkuti, who has died aged 79, was the deep-lying Hungarian centre-forward of the 1950s remembered for his hat-trick at Wembley in November 1953, when Hungary won 6-3 and England's long unbeaten home record against foreign teams was broken. The most traumatising goal was the first, scored in less than 90 seconds. Receiving the ball outside the English penalty area with sufficient time and space, Hidegkuti swerved to wrong-foot the England centre-half Harry Johnston, then smashed a right-footed drive past the goalkeeper Gil Merrick.

Hidegkuti learned his football in the backstreets of his native Budapest. He was a rarity in the Hungarian team since he was not co-opted for the Honved army team, remaining instead with MTK of Budapest, which changed its name for some years to Voros Lobogo (Red Banner). When Hungary won the Helsinki Olympic tournament in 1952, Hidegkuti was an outside-right. But his value was shown the following September, when Hungary met Switzerland in Berne. Gustav Sebes, the deputy sports minister, who presided over the squad, decided that Peter Palotas, in the deep centre-forward role, had done so well in the Olympics that he would keep him there.

Hidegkuti started as a substitute. Strictly at that time they were not allowed but this was a friendly so, when the Swiss went 2-0 ahead within 30 minutes, Hidegkuti replaced Palotas. As Sebes recalled: 'He seemed to complement that partnership between [Ferenc] Puskas and [Sandor] Kocsis perfectly and beautiful passes began to flow between the three of them. Before half-time Hidegkuti had laid two goals on for Puskas." Hungary won 4-2.

In May 1953, when Hungary beat Italy 3-0 in Rome, those lucky enough to be there could appreciate Hidegkuti's balance, skill, flair and intelligence. 'I played Hidegkuti,' remembered Sebes, 'even though he was only half fit, because I needed his fine technique and tactical guile to penetrate the world's toughest defence.'

At Wembley that November England were baffled by his role, giving him too much room and time. Johnston came off at half-time complaining that he had not even touched the ball. Later he claimed he had never been told how to play Hidegkuti, though Walter Winterbottom, the team manager, denied it. Either way, Hidegkuti ran riot. When England, fleetingly, were level at 1-1, he put Hungary ahead again with a rocketing shot and he scored their sixth goal in the second half.

'Neither the English nor any of the other teams we met seemed able to defend effectively against our tactical formation,' he recalled. 'If [right-half] Jozsef Bozsik and I joined the attack, we had six strikers advancing, all capable of scoring goals. We used to joke with our defenders sometimes: "Don't worry if you let one in, we'll score two." That's how we felt.'

The Hungarian team greatly enjoyed the passage home. 'We were allowed to stay in Paris for two days,' Hidegkuti said, 'which was a rare treat. We went to a match and, when the crowd learned we were there, they began to shout for us to go on the pitch before the game started, which we did. Some of the crowd wanted the original match abandoned and us to play one half against each team."

Hidegkuti maintained his form in the 7-1 crushing of England in Budapest the following May and, in the ensuing World Cup finals in Switzerland, he scored against West Germany in an 8-3 win. In the quarter-finals against Brazil, the so-called 'Battle of Berne', he crashed a corner into the net in the third minute, having his shorts torn off him as he did so. Five minutes later his centre enabled Kocsis to head in Hungary's second goal on their way to a 4-2 win. The match degenerated into a brawl, though Hidegkuti was not involved. An epic semi-final against Uruguay in Lausanne followed, in which Hidegkuti scored with a header, though there was nothing even he could do to save Hungary as they dramatically lost the final 3-2 to the Germans in Berne.

Though Hidegkuti played in Hungary's first game of the World Cup finals in Stockholm four years later, he looked slow and obsolescent. After 63 games for his country he took over Italy's Fiorentina as manager in 1960, then Mantova. On his return to Hungary he managed unfashionable Vasas Gyor, winning the national championship. One of his two sons went on to play for Voros Lobogo.

Nandor Hidegkuti, born March 3 1922, died February 14 2002

Three-nation star

LADISLAO KUBALA

The only treble international in soccer history, Ladislao Kubala, who has died after a long illness aged 74, was a thick-thighed, blond, muscular, cheerfully heavy drinker, who allied exceptional skill with tactical flair and a devastating right-footed shot with which he scored two goals against England for the Fifa XI at Wembley in October 1953, one of them from a penalty kick.

A precocious talent, who began playing league football at 15 and was a Hungarian international two years later, he won 11 caps for the Czech national team and also played for Spain. He will be best remembered for his years with Barcelona where, despite constantly harsh treatment from opponents, which led to no fewer than seven knee operations, he became an idol, having managed to escape from behind the Iron Curtain.

Born to parents of Czech origin in Budapest – his father was a bricklayer, his mother a factory hand – Kubala joined the local Ferencvaros club and, as an 18-year-old in 1945, scored 19 league goals for them. The next year he moved with his family to

Czechoslovakia and joined Slovan Bratislava, who used him as a centre-forward, though later he would be best known as an inside-right.

In 1948 he returned to Budapest to play for Vasas as an inside-forward, altogether playing three times for Hungary. But he longed to escape from the communist regime and, although he had just signed a contract with Vasas, he managed to get out of the country in January 1949, first to an American zone in Austria, then to Busto Arsizio in Italy, where he initially joined the local Pro Patria club, then a Serie A side.

The Hungarians protested to Fifa, demanding his extradition on various disputable charges, among them evading military service, and Fifa banned him for a year. So, in January 1950 Kubala went to another American transit camp, at Cinecitta, the home of Italian film production outside Rome, where he formed Hungaria, a touring team with other exiles, and even made a film about them, subsequently called Kubala: Stars in Search of Peace. The team found its way to Spain, where Kubala evoked the admiration and support of Pepe Samitier, Barcelona's former star centre-forward, who became anxious to keep him away from Real Madrid, the rival team equally keen for a signing. According to legend, Samitier put Kubala on a train to Barcelona, persuading him, after abundant libations, that he was actually going to Madrid to sign for Real.

Once in Barcelona Kubala managed to get the same generous terms he had in his unsigned deal with Real Madrid. But it was nine months before the Fifa ban was lifted and, under the managership of his father-in-law, the Slovak Fernando Daucik, Kubala became a Barcelona star, vilified and maltreated elsewhere in Spain.

Well paid, generous to a fault, he was soon an icon in Barcelona, helping the club to its most successful spell for years.

In his post-playing days he would coach their juniors, then the club itself, but never with the same success. Indeed he lost the job in 1963, distressing fans by playing, for a while, with their historic rivals, the lesser team of Barcelona, Espanyol, alongside that other great player who slipped through Barcelona's hands, Alfredo di Stéfano.

Kubala's Barcelona debut came in two friendly games against West Germany's Frankfurt, in which he scored six goals and helped to make five. 'The public came out of these games in a state of amazement,' said a local paper. Kubala continued to amaze them for years.

As a naturalised Spaniard he won another 15 caps for his new country, scoring 11 goals in all. But when Spain played Turkey in Rome in 1954, the winner of the play-off to qualify for the World Cup in Switzerland, a faked cable from Fifa put him out of the match and Spain lost.

Kubala was also a star of the Spanish championship, the cup, the Inter-Cities Fairs Cup and the old Latin Cup. But when the volatile Helenio Herrera arrived as manager in 1958, things inevitably began to go wrong. Herrera, an Argentinian brought up in Casablanca, was a rampaging egotist who brooked no rivals. Kubala was openly scathing about the semi-mystical rituals which Herrera imposed on the team before each game. In the 1959-60 season the two quarrelled bitterly over bonuses. Kubala was dropped from the European Cup semi-finals against Real Madrid, who prevailed.

Herrera resigned after being attacked in the street. The following season Kubala made the goal which gave Barcelona European Cup revenge against Real. In the final in Berne, against Benfica, he hit the post twice but Benfica won and he retired.

He would successively manage Espanyol, Elch and FC Zurich, for whom he once played in a European Cup tie against Celtic at the age of 39. Then his peregrinations continued. In the summer of 1967, big and slow by now, he played in Yankee stadium with his son for Toronto Falcons against the New York Generals in an unofficial professional league.

After that he went back to Spain to coach Cordoba. Success was limited but, though the club was relegated, in July 1969 Kubala was appointed manager of the Spanish international team on a three-year contract. Between 1969 and 1980 he coached them for 68 games. Again, however, success was limited, as indeed it had been with the Canadian national team and was to be in Saudi Arabia.

Kubala will be remembered as a superb player and a remarkable, somewhat Rabelaisian, personality, above all in his beloved Barcelona, where he eventually retired, still playing veterans' football on those cruelly damaged knees. Of him that other great exile in Spain, Alfredo di Stéfano, said: 'Kubala was one of the best there has ever been. His game was pure, crystalline, a real joy for the fans. What I remember is his spirit of comradeship, the loyalty he showed as a friend.'

Ladislao Kubala, born June 10 1927, died May 17 2002

APRIL 14 2005

French history-maker

LUCIEN LAURENT

Lucien Laurent scored the first goal at the inaugural World Cup finals on July 13 1930, in Montevideo, for France against Mexico. Sixty-eight years later, at the age of 90, he was the last survivor of that French team and able to attend the World Cup finals, which

France won on their own soil. He was still lively, lucid and cogent, with a clear memory of what went on before and during that initial World Cup.

Indeed, had he not been injured by a brutal foul from the Argentinian centre-half Luisito Monti early in France's second game, his team might have made further progress. There were no substitutes in those days, Laurent's ankle injury reduced him to being a passenger and France lost 1-0.

Laurent, who has died aged 97, was born in Saint Maur, in the Val de Marne, one of two brothers who both played for France. Jean, the elder, also went to Montevideo but did not get a game. Lucien's first club was CAP (Cercle Athlétique de Paris), which he joined as a boy in 1921, remaining with them for nine years. An inside-right, he was 5ft 4in and 10st 3lb – an advantage, he would joke in his old age, when he, the rest of the French team and several other European squads were all crammed into the ship that took them to Uruguay.

By then he had recently transferred to Peugeot Sochaux, the club subsidised by the Peugeot factory where he worked. He was given time off to play in the World Cup but was not paid while away. Indeed, as an amateur he received only basic expenses from the French federation. Three other players from Peugeot made the trip, Lucien's brother, Etienne Mattler and Andre Maschinot.

In those days it took three weeks to reach South America from Europe, a fact that discouraged the big European battalions – Austria, Hungary, Italy and Spain – from making the trip. But Laurent enjoyed it immensely, finding plenty to do on the boat which included among its passengers the Belgian, Romanian and Yugoslav squads. The French trained in the morning and were entertained later by a violinist and a comedian. Laurent spent much of his time in the cinema or in the swimming pool. 'It was like a holiday camp,' he said.

His great regret was that, in Montevideo itself, he could not play in the imposing new Centenary Stadium. It had not been finished and earlier matches took place on club grounds. It was winter in Uruguay and on the day of the opening match against Mexico it was snowing. A long clearance by the agile French goalkeeper Alex Thepot was controlled by Augustin Chantrel, who launched the right-winger, Ernest Liberati on a dash to the goalline. When the ball was pulled back Laurent, on the edge of the penalty box, struck home with his right foot. France went on to win 4-1.

Against Argentina the French were underdogs but, despite Monti's foul on Laurent, they grew in confidence as the game went on, ultimately conceding the solitary goal from Monti's free-kick after 81 minutes. Three minutes later the referee mistakenly blew for full time. But the referee, Almeida Rego of Brazil, acknowledged his error, the teams returned and the final minutes were played out after a quarter-hour hiatus. Laurent's injury kept him out of France's third match, against Chile.

Overall he played 10 times for France, scoring one other goal. His debut was against Portugal in Porto in February 1930, a 2-0 defeat. In May brother Jean played three successive games for France at right-half, in which Lucien did not figure, only for their fortunes to be reversed in the opening World Cup match against Mexico. Lucien then played the following March in a 1-0 win at the Stade Colombes in Paris against Germany.

In May 1931 Laurent was a member of the French team that thrashed England 5-2 and he was recalled to the colours for his final cap as late as May 1935 when, at Colombes, he was once more inside-left in a 2-0 victory over the Hungarians.

His clubs were many and various. After two years at Sochaux he went to the long defunct Club Français for a year, back to CAP for another and, for a season each, to Mulhouse, Sochaux and Rennes.

He went to Strasbourg in 1937-38 but early in the war he was taken prisoner and put in a camp in Saxony. On his return he found the possessions he had placed in a furniture depository in Strasbourg had been stolen by the Germans, including his 1930 World Cup jersey.

'Happily,' he said in 1998, 'all my memories were there, well established in a corner of my old head. No one can steal those from me.' He looked back then on the day when he was ball boy at the old Pershing stadium at Vincennes, when France beat Belgium 2-1 and his heroes, Paul Nicolas and Lucien Gamblin were playing. He had a son, Marc.

Lucien Laurent, born December 10 1907, died April 11 2005

NOVEMBER 6 2007

Honed on pine needles

NILS LIEDHOLM

The Swedish-born Nils Liedholm, who has died aged 85, was one of the finest footballers of his day, winning four Italian Championship titles with AC Milan, captaining Sweden's World Cup final team in 1958 and later becoming one of Italy's most successful club managers.

There was always something of the altruist about Liedholm. This was displayed when, after doing his military service and with a coruscating football career before him, he redeemed a promise to a fellow conscript and went off to play for three years for an obscure Second Division club, AL Sleipner. Three times the club came second in the league, inspired by Liedholm's performances at inside-left, before Lajos Czeizler persuaded him to join IFK Norrköpping.

It was the beginning of a sustained period of success as Liedholm teamed up with the equally celebrated Gunnar Nordahl, a powerfully built centre-forward. The two played harmoniously together and remained friends.

Liedholm had been born in Valdermarsvik and as a young amateur he played not only football but ice hockey. He skied and ran across pine needles to strengthen his calves. He worked for a small salary in a lawyer's office. Tall, athletic and well-built, with a notable left foot, a strong shot, an ability to dribble – never to be shown off more spectacularly than in the 1958 World Cup final against Brazil in Stockholm – Liedholm was also a fine passer of the ball and an excellent strategist. He endlessly worked on his skills – inside and outside of the foot, kicking with the instep over distances, short passes.

In 1948 he came to London with Sweden's Olympic team. It possessed so much talent that there was no room for him in the inside-forward trio. At inside-left played the fair-haired Garuis Carlsson and the other two inside-forwards were Nordahl and Gunnar Gren, so Liedholm was obliged to move to the left wing. The Swedes eventually won the tournament, beating Yugoslavia 3-1 in the final at Wembley. Then the Italian clubs swooped and Liedholm and Nordahl were on their way to Milan, where Gren would join them the following season. It was no coincidence that in the 1950-51 season Milan won the Italian Championship for the first time for 40 years. They won it again in 1955, 1957 and 1959.

In the return leg European Cup semi-final of 1958, against a Manchester United team depleted by the Munich air disaster, Liedholm bestrode the field. United had won the first leg 2-1 at Old Trafford but Liedholm, scoring himself and creating two goals for Juan Schiaffino, was irresistible that night and Milan won 4-0.

They almost won the final in Brussels against a Real Madrid side that had won the two previous European Cups. Liedholm had a superb match again, operating at inside-right, with Schiaffino used at centre-forward. Real narrowly survived normal time and won with a goal in the 107th minute.

Liedholm then went off to play in the World Cup for Sweden, who were now at last using professionals. George Raynor, the English team manager, had been in charge of Sweden's team when Liedholm first played for it. Liedholm, despite his 35 years, was as effective at inside-left as the veteran Gren, at 37, was at inside-right. 'We're the slowest team in the competition,' observed Raynor. 'If there was a relay race between all the teams, Sweden would finish last. But we'll still reach the final.'

So they did but the hand of Liedholm played a part. In the semi-final against West Germany in Gothenburg he clearly brought the ball down with his hand but got away with it, to set up the Swedish equaliser for 'Nacka' Skoglund. They won 3-1 and, as Raynor promised, went on to the final in Stockholm.

Raynor made another forecast, not fulfilled: 'If Brazil give away an early goal, they'll panic all over the show.' Brazil did indeed give away an early goal but they refused to panic and eventually won easily. Liedholm himself scored that goal after four minutes and it looked too easy to be true. Accepting a pass from Gren, he surged into the penalty area, beat two defenders and shot past Gilmar. Illusions were roused. But Brazil won the match 5-2.

Liedholm was still a young man when, in 1961, he gave up playing. Milan gave him a job as coach to the juniors, then in 1964 made him their manager. In 1971 he went to Fiorentina, using largely the same 4-4-2 tactics he had employed with Milan. There he promoted the careers of gifted teenagers, among them Giancarlo Antognoni, who would become the pivot in midfield of the Italian national team. 'What a championship,' Liedholm later recalled. 'We only came fourth but the Florentine fans still remember certain spectacular games.' In 1973 he began his first spell with Roma, where again he promoted gifted youngsters. He later moved several times between that club and Milan.

In 1978-79 he won the Championship with Milan and repeated the feat four years later with Roma, playing zonally. The following season Roma reached the European Cup final, only to lose on penalties in their own stadium to Liverpool. In 1984-85 Liedholm was back with Milan, where he had the Englishmen Mark Hateley and Ray Wilkins in his charge. On retirement he cultivated a vineyard in Piedmont, northern Italy, with his son, Carlo.

Nils Liedholm, born October 8 1922, died November 5 2007

MAY 15 2002

Cutting-edge coach

VALERI LOBANOVSKY

Valeri Lobanovsky, who has died aged 63 following brain surgery, was for more than a quarter of a century one of the world's most influential and innovative football coaches. Though he might have seemed an authoritarian figure at Dynamo Kiev, where he worked both before and after the demise of the Soviet Union, he deprecated any such idea, insisting that football had evolved to a point where no one man could cope with all its aspects, so that he needed a team of experts to assist him. He also managed the Soviet Union team in the 1986 and 1990 World Cup finals.

Born in Kiev, in the then Ukrainian Soviet republic, Lobanovsky turned Dynamo Kiev into a team of remarkable skill and talent, climaxing first when, with a superb display of cultured football, they beat Ferencvaros of Hungary in the 1975 European Cup-Winners' Cup final, the first Soviet team to win a major European competition, and chosen almost *en bloc* to represent the Soviet Union in the European Championship and World Cups.

Before Ukraine obtained independence there was bitter rivalry between Dynamo Kiev and their Muscovite opponents. But Lobanovsky rose above such conflicts. 'My habit,' he said, 'is to distance myself from non-sports situations. When I prepared my players for an important match, I never told them that they had to win at all costs because they were playing a Moscow team. If the players will not give of their best in a match of that kind, they can't hope to win.'

On the first occasion he took the Soviet Union to the World Cup Lobanovsky filled the team with his Kiev players and led them to the second round in Mexico, where they were surprisingly beaten by Belgium. With perestroika, however, it at last became possible for star Soviet players to go abroad and earn the kind of money they had never dreamed of at home, and Dynamo Kiev lost most of their top men to West German and Italian teams. So, by the 1990 World Cup finals in Italy Lobanovsky, though still in charge at Kiev, had to bring his former players from far and wide. No longer did he have them under his intense control and the Soviet team had a disappointing tournament.

After this anticlimax he then went off to some surprise to seek his fortune in the Middle East, initially managing the Arab Emirates team. 'It was a new challenge,' he said, 'a chance to have a different professional experience, to open up new horizons.' But he was sacked in 1994 and moved on to the undistinguished Kuwait team where, as he admitted, the unpaid players could not even be guaranteed to turn up for training or to play.

Two years later, with eight months still to run on his contract,

Lobanovsky was dismissed again, with his team of assistants. Sheikh Ahmed Al Fahd, a Kuwaiti government minister and member of the International Olympic Committee, wanted to keep him, pointing out that Kuwait still had a chance of qualifying for the Asian Nations Cup. But the ruling commission was implacable, asserting that 'Lobanovsky has turned the players into robots. He has killed both entertainment and creativity.'

So, in January 1997, older, richer and plumper, Lobanovsky went back to Kiev, a club now Ukrainian rather than Soviet, and in deep crisis. Charged by Uefa, the European ruling body, with a crude attempt to bribe the Spanish referee Laez Nieto, they had been thrown out of European competition, though the club was subsequently reprieved. Violent incidents had beset officials and the team was struggling to assert itself.

Lobanovsky quickly showed he had lost none of his old touch. When it was said to him that the team had fallen on hard times, he replied that every side had its ups and downs. 'But Dynamo lives. It has its traditions, its good foundations and the potential to set off again to conquer the summits. It also has the will.'

Things improved with astounding speed. True to his beliefs, Lobanovsky assembled a team of assistants. Michael Ochemko had a leading administrative role – his father, when manager of Dynamo Kiev, had launched Lobanovsky on his own career as a coach. The two of them travelled extensively. The days of Oleg Blokhin and the 1970s team were remote, as were the days of Alexiy Mikhailichenko, Igor Belanov and Aleksandr Zavarov. But now there were new stars, such as the attackers Sergei Rebrov and Andriy Shevchenko. With Lobanovsky to inspire them, this Dynamo Kiev team bade fair to equal its famous predecessors. By the European Champions Cup of 1997-78 Kiev were not merely champions of Ukraine but competed strongly against Europe's best, twice humiliating Barcelona.

For Lobanovsky modern football meant speed and power and players' technique needed to be of the highest quality. He rejected the term total football, as applied to the brilliant Dutch and West German teams of the mid-1970s, and said that he would never expect, say, a centre-forward to perform the role of a defender or vice versa. When these players found themselves in such a different position, however, they should be capable of mastering it.

A voracious student of football magazines, match videos and scientific studies, Lobanovsky believed that psychology was as important as the physical side of the game. 'I don't just speak of the sporting aspect of things,' he declared. 'I'm equally inspired by scientific theories, which enable me to plan the training sessions, or by philosophical ideas, which allow me to organise the group of which I have charge. Every manager in the world says that the most difficult thing of all is the leadership of men. They are right but do they know that reading philosophical works can help us?'

For Lobanovsky 'the time of absolute power and authoritarian decisions seems to me to have gone and I know that acting on this basis I can question myself more and, above all, renew my ideas'.

In February 1998 he was appointed manager of the Ukrainian national team, in succession to his protégé Jozef Scabo.

Valeri Lobanovsky, born January 6 1939, died May 13 2002

Total success

RINUS MICHELS

Rinus Michels, the Dutch coach who laid the basis for what, in the early 1970s, became known as 'total football', has died after complications from heart surgery, aged 77. The true architect of the famous Holland and Ajax teams of the 1970s and 1980s, he had similar success with Barcelona. Though he never, as a manager, won a World Cup, he and his protégé, the coruscating centre-forward Johan Cruyff, could hardly have come closer than they did in Munich in 1974.

Michels was a centre-forward of no mean attributes, making an extraordinary debut for Ajax, the club in his home town of Amsterdam, as an 18-year-old in June 1946. Ajax defeated ADO in The Hague 8-3, Michels scoring five. He went on to play in 10 Dutch championship matches that season, scoring seven goals, though Ajax were pipped to the title by Haarlem. The following season, thanks in no small measure to Michels' goals, they won it.

In March 1950 Michels was among the Ajax stars who took part in the Ajax in Gold 50th anniversary revue, though the season ended in anticlimax when, in May, his club lost an away game against Heerenveen 6-5, having been 5-1 ahead. Dutch football then was still all-amateur. Michels played 269 times for Ajax and scored 121 goals. He won another Championship medal in 1957 and five caps. He retired to become a gymnastics teacher.

Then, in January 1965, Ajax dismissed their jaunty English coach Vic Buckingham and appointed Michels in his place. The Ajax season had gone badly until then but three days later

Michels, the first full-time Dutch manager, made a spectacular start, with his new charges beating MVV 9-3.

With the 17-year-old Cruyff emerging as an astonishing talent, Ajax went from strength to strength under Michels' stern regime. In December 1966, in a European Cup match at their Olympic stadium, they thrashed the English champions, Liverpool, 5-1, eliciting from Liverpool's manager, Bill Shankly, the memorable response that it was sad to see a home team playing so defensively.

Piet Keizer, the gifted Ajax outside-left, reflected: 'When Michels took over he changed the playing staff considerably and he changed the training even more. His was the hardest physical preparation I ever had. We sometimes had four sessions a day. He also introduced the Italian system of taking the players away for a period of concentrated training before a big match. We would start work in the morning and carry on until the evening. He was by no means a miserable man but he was very strict with the players and there were lots of arguments about discipline. The message was pretty clear that those who did not like it would have to leave.'

Michels, whose classically Dutch features, with obdurate nose and chin, would not have looked out of place in a Rembrandt, embraced a squad system, with 16 or so players to choose from. He encouraged his full-backs to attack and the underlying philosophy of 'total football' was one of complete versatility. He led Ajax to the Dutch Championship in 1966, 1967, 1968 and 1970 and took the Dutch Cup in 1967, 1970 and 1971.

Ajax got to the European Cup final in Madrid in 1969 but their team had yet to reach its peak and Milan won 4-1. Of Michels his left-back Theo van Duivenbode said: 'He was an expert in planning the tactics before a match and preparing players physically and mentally.' After Madrid Michels sold Van Duivenbode and brought in the more powerful Ruud Krol, who would also excel as a sweeper.

Two years later Ajax won the European Cup final, easily beating the Greeks of Panathinaikos at Wembley, and Michels promptly left them for Barcelona. The new coach, the Romanian Stefan Kovacs, responded more sympathetically to his players' demands for increased flexibility and the 'total football' team went on to win two more European Cups, in 1972 and 1973.

Meanwhile the Dutch national team qualified for the World Cup finals in West Germany but, with its players clamouring for more money, all was chaos until Michels took over. Calm and discipline were quickly restored and a brilliant Dutch side, inspired by Cruyff and the forceful Johan Neeskens, swept to the final. Had Barry Hulshoff, who had been Michels' centre-half at Ajax, been fit, had the Dutch not relaxed after scoring so early, had Johnny Rep not missed an easy chance before half-time, perhaps Holland would have won. In the event they were beaten 2-1 by the host country. But had Michels not taken over, telling dissident players that those not satisfied with the financial terms could stay behind, it is doubtful if the Dutch would have got as far as they did.

Under Michels' aegis Ajax set up a coaching system which became the envy of the world game. Boys joined it to be expertly coached and carefully supervised to full maturity. Technique was prized and promoted.

In June 1988 Michels was sufficiently recovered from heart surgery to take charge of Holland in the European Championship finals, also in West Germany. Surprisingly he omitted the outstanding centre-forward Marco van Basten, Cruyff's natural heir at Ajax, from the line-up against Russia in the opening game. Admittedly Van Basten, by then with AC Milan, had missed most of that season through injury but he had returned impressively for the last few games. Holland lost 1-0. Restored to the Dutch team, Van Basten made an immediate impact and in the final in Munich, again against the Russians, scored a stupendous right-footed volleyed goal from an acute angle. With other Milan stars in Ruud Gullit and Frank Rijkaard resplendent, Holland triumphed 2-0.

Two years later Michels, still working for the Dutch federation, was not in charge of the team that went to the 1990 World Cup finals in Italy. The job went to Leo Beenhakker, a less authoritarian coach, but Michels went along with the squad and it may have been some resulting tension that undermined the Dutch performance. The team laboured through the qualifying stages before going down against West Germany 2-1 in an exciting second-round match. But there is no doubt that Michels, over the years, was the dominant figure in Dutch football. In 1999 he was named Fifa coach of the century.

Marinus Hendrikus Jacobus Michels, born February 9 1928, died March 3 2005

JANUARY 31 2003

Bohemian tearaway

MILOS MILUTINOVIC

Though the fame of the Yugoslav footballer Milos Milutinovic, who has died aged 69, was eclipsed by that of his brother Bora in later years, there is no doubt which was the better player. Both played in France and latterly Mexico. Bora was a solid centre-half but Milos, who scored 16 goals in 34 international games, having switched from outside-right to centre-forward, was a coruscating star, fast and elusive and with remarkable ball control.

He was born at Bajina Basta in Serbia and, growing to 5ft 11in and 12st plus, was not easily forced off the ball. Beginning his career with the Bor club, he moved to Partizan of Belgrade, where he initially established himself as a centre-forward. Later he played in West Germany for Bayern Munich, in France for the Racing Club and eventually in Mexico City.

In 1954 he inspired the Yugoslav attack in the World Cup finals in Switzerland. He was used at outside-right, where his speed and control had ample scope. In the opening game, against France, he scored the only goal of the match. In his country's second game, against Brazil, again in Lausanne – a match of the highest quality, ending in a 1-1 draw – Milutinovic might have settled the match when sent through by Dionizije Dvornic but was thwarted by Carlos Jose Castilho's brave dive at his feet. The quarter-finals in Geneva saw Yugoslavia defeated 2-0 by West Germany.

The following year, after France and Yugoslavia had drawn 1-1 in Paris, a leading French football journalist wrote that Milutinovic 'seems to be individually the best Yugoslav footballer since the Liberation. He possessed absolutely the whole arsenal of the great attacker. Unfortunately his collective spirit is not yet at the level of his individual possibilities.'

Shortly before the 1958 World Cup in Sweden Milutinovic led a Yugoslav attack in Belgrade that devastated England 5-0, scoring the first himself. In Sweden he was centre-forward in the 1-1 draw with Scotland in Västerås and the 3-2 win against France at the same ground. He returned to centre-forward in the quarter-finals but a goal by the powerful German right-winger Helmut Rahn decided the game 1-0.

After retiring Milutinovic became for a time manager of the Yugoslav national side. Married to a Yugoslav woman, he had a daughter who was born in Germany. A French football magazine succinctly described his character as 'artist, bohemian'.

Milos Milutinovic, born February 5 1933, died January 28 2003

MARCH 24 2000

Flying bicyclist

CARLO PAROLA

Carlo Parola, who has died aged 78, won only 10 caps for Italy but he will long be remembered there as one of the most elegant and accomplished centre-halves of his time. He was also, at 26, the only Italian in the Rest of Europe team that lost 6-1 to Britain at Hampden Park in May 1947.

This was a game in which Parola was unfortunate enough to put through his own goal for Britain's fifth. Yet, in a team hastily cobbled together from a plethora of nationalities, he stood out for his aplomb and cool command and for his reverse, over-the-head bicycle kick, now a standard weapon in the footballers' armoury.

As Parola recalled years later: 'I was at once complimented by the managers and by my team-mates for my famous flying bicycle kick, which had the effect of putting an opponent off his stroke, the ball being whipped away from under his nose when he thought he had full control of it. I was [then] very good in antici-pation and in guessing my opponents' moves in advance. I felt full of energy but I could not, logically, be everywhere at once when danger threatened.'

Though he joined Lazio of Rome in 1954, aged 33, Parola had by then lost his pace and it was sad to see so fine a player struggling to compete. At 38 he returned to Juventus, the club with which he had excelled, as manager, flanked by their former Argentinian star Renato Cesarini, but he was not destined for success in management.

His debut for Juve had come when he was 18. His first international appearance was made against Hungary in Turin in 1942 but his full international debut did not come until November 1945 when, in Zurich, he played against Switzerland in a 4-4 draw. He was in Turin again, in May 1948, when England defeated Italy 4-0, but two years later, in Sao Paulo, he met his nemesis, in the shape of the forceful Swedish centre-forward, Hans Jeppson.

In the World Cup qualifying rounds Italy had been drawn against the Swedes and were favoured to beat a team so much reduced by departures of star players abroad, chiefly to Italy. But Jeppson gave Parola a torrid time, scoring twice in a 3-2 victory, and Parola would never play for his country again.

The journalist and historian Antonio Ghirelli wrote of him: 'The man of Glasgow, as he came to be called, effectively represented the most complete example of the third-back defender. Coming out of the ranks of the northern working-class, brought up in the technical and style school of Juventus, tall, slim and robust in person, alien to any harshness in contact, more inclined to the acrobatic and the elegant, rich in commitment and fair play, master of ball control like few others and always looking for the constructive pass, rather than the hasty clearance ...' He added that 'you couldn't name a formation player more harmonious than Parola' but 'his weakness, naturally exacerbated by his physical decline, lay, if anything, in an excess of sportsmanship and in a certain elegant exhibitionism, both prejudicial defects in the modern game.'

Parola played 35 out of 38 games for Juventus when they won the Italian Championship in 1949-50 and 15 when they won it again in 1951-2.

Carlo Parola, born September 20 1921, died March 22 2000

OCTOBER 5 1996

Italy's foxy forward

SILVIO PIOLA

Silvio Piola, who has died aged 83, was one of the best Italian centre-forwards of all time and perhaps the best in the 1938 World Cup finals in France, when his goals were crucial in winning Italy the title. Yet in England he will be remembered chiefly for two controversial incidents in games between Italy and England.

The first was in May 1939 in Milan, when a long pass down the middle was punched by Piola into the English goal. Pecos Bauwens, the German referee, immediately gave a goal. To add injury to insult Piola followed through and punched the England right-back, George Male, in the eye, though Male was always eager to maintain this was an accident.

Long afterwards Piola, who had been attending a coaches' conference in Florence and was sitting at a cafe table in the Piazza della Repubblica, showed how he did it. Having first laughingly called it 'that header' he aimed a punch over his shoulder and admitted 'No, ho fatto cosi!' (Hey! I did it like this.)

In 1952, again in Florence, he had surprisingly been recalled at the age of 38 after a long absence to lead Italy's attack against England. He looked sadly static. But Jack Froggatt, England's centre-half, wearied by Piola's frequent use of his elbows, eventually kicked him, bringing a fine international career to an inglorious end.

Tall, gangling, with a prominent, much caricatured nose, Piola made his name with the once celebrated Pro Vercelli club, for whom he made his debut in the 1929-30 season. He scored 51 league goals in the next four seasons, exploiting his strength, his power in the air, his adroit technique and his strong shooting.

He moved in 1934 to Lazio of Rome, where he had his finest eight years, staying with them until after the war, when he went to Juventus, having played in the wartime championship for their city rivals Torino. In 1948 Piola moved again, to the less fashionable Novara, where he ended his first-class career.

He made his debut for Italy in demanding circumstances on March 24 1935 in Vienna against their eternal rivals Austria. Italy won 2-0 with Piola scoring both goals. In all he would play in 33 internationals, scoring a remarkable 30 goals. His great rival for the Italian centre-forward position and the title of most prolific Italian goalscorer of the era was Giuseppe Meazza of Internazionale. But Vittorio Pozzo, Italy's overlord, resolved any potential problem by using Meazza as inside-right. It was thus that Italy won the 1938 World Cup in France.

Major Frank Buckley, the legendary manager of Wolverhampton Wanderers, had eulogised Piola as early as 1933 after a tournament in Nice. 'Piola will be the best centre-forward in Europe shortly,' Buckley predicted, and he was proved abundantly right.

In Italy's opening game in the 1938 World Cup they struggled desperately against Norway in Marseilles. The match went to extra-time but five minutes later, when the Norwegian goalkeeper failed to hold a shot, Piola followed up to score.

Against France in Paris in the next round he was irresistible. 'Piola,' wrote a critic, 'opened up the game for his forwards with the left foot, right foot, head, it made no difference. He was in constant action, always moving to receive the ball at just the right moment, quietly slipping to the wings when heavily marked. He had surprising suddenness of movement and liveliness of action with head and legs, understandable in an athlete but astonishing in a person of his square build and height.'

Piola scored two in the second half and, in the semi-final against Brazil in Marseilles, he so enraged the Brazilian defender Domingos with his elusiveness and elbows that Domingos brutally fouled him and was sent off. It was a penalty and Meazza scored from it. In the final in Paris against Hungary Piola scored Italy's second and fourth goals in a 4-2 victory.

For many years he and Meazza ran neck and neck as Italy's top goalscorers but Piola outlasted Meazza and went ahead when he scored for Novara Como in February 1951, taking his total to 356. After retirement he became the first manager of the Italian Under-23 team which beat England's Under-23s 3-0 in Bologna in 1954.

Silvio Piola, born September 29 1913, died October 4 1996

NOVEMBER 18 2006

Galloping Major

FERENC PUSKAS

The remarkable career of Ferenc Puskas, who has died aged 79 in Budapest, falls into two parts. The first was as the outstanding captain of an extraordinary Hungarian team – once called 'the best in the world' by England's Billy Wright – which he led to the World Cup final of 1954. The second was as a star of Real Madrid from 1958 to 1966.

The watershed was the Hungarian revolution of 1956 when, by chance, Puskas and other Hungarian internationals were on tour with Honved, the army club into which most of them had been drafted. Puskas, possessed of a left foot of astonishing power, and his team-mates, Sandor Kocsis and Zoltan Czibor, all found their way to Spain. Puskas joined Real, with the other two joining Barcelona.

Puskas was born in Budapest and brought up in the nearby country town of Kispest. The son of a footballer, he kicked a ball about in the streets with, among others, the future Hungary right-half, Josef Bozsik, and admired such foreign stars as Charlie Buchan, Ted Drake and Spain's celebrated goalkeeper, Ricardo Zamora. Nicknamed 'Ocsi' (little brother), Puskas made his debut in November 1943 against the then league leaders, Nagyvared.

An inside-left from the beginning, he perfected his ball skills by endlessly juggling with a tennis ball. At 18 he won the first of his 84 caps for Hungary, scoring the first of his 83 goals. When Kispest was swallowed up by Honved, Puskas was commissioned in the army – hence his eventual nickname, the Galloping Major – though, like most such army footballers, he was seldom to be seen on parade.

For some years a brilliant Hungarian team was kept under wraps behind the Iron Curtain but in the summer of 1952 it finally emerged to waltz through the Olympic football tournament in Helsinki. They beat Yugoslavia 2-0 in the final and, although Puskas missed a penalty, he atoned by scoring in open play.

In May 1953 Hungary took part in the first game in the new Olympic stadium in Rome with a superb performance, beating Italy 3-0. The following November, unforgettably, they came to London and thrashed England 6-3, becoming the first foreign team to beat England at Wembley. Puskas scored two of the goals, one coming when he coolly pulled the ball back with the sole of his boot so that, in the words of Geoffrey Green in *The Times*, the English captain Billy Wright was left lunging 'like a fire engine going to the wrong fire'.

Inevitably Hungary were favourites to win the World Cup in Switzerland in June 1954. They might have done so had Puskas, in the opening 8-3 win over West Germany, not been injured in a tackle by the German centre-half, Werner Liebrich. This might have been the kick that won West Germany the cup.

Hungary regrouped to great effect but, when the team eventually reached the final in Berne, Puskas insisted he should play. He also, reportedly, demanded that the right-winger, Laszlo Budai, be dropped. In the event Puskas did not look fully fit. Even so, with Hungary 3-2 behind after squandering a 2-0 lead, he raced through the opposing defence to score what looked like a perfectly good goal. But the Welsh linesman, Mervyn Griffiths, waved his flag and the English referee, Bill Ling, ruled Puskas offside. He remained convinced that he was not.

During his years with Real Madrid an increasingly tubby but still marvellously effective Puskas struck up a famous partnership with the Argentinian centre-forward, the domineering Alfredo Di Stéfano. Puskas became the leading Spanish goalscorer four times, in 1960, 1961, 1963 and 1964. Both he and Di Stéfano triumphed in the European Cup final of 1960 in Hampden Park, Glasgow, where Eintracht Frankfurt were famously demolished 7-3. Puskas scored four goals, Di Stéfano three.

Two years later Puskas got another three in the European Cup final in Amsterdam against Benfica and finished on the losing side. Benfica won 5-3 but the goal Puskas scored when Di Stéfano cleverly put him through from the halfway line was as good as any that night. It was reported that at the end of the match, in a symbolic gesture, Puskas took off his jersey and gave it to Eusebio, the young Mozambique inside-right whose thunderous right foot was the equal of Puskas's left. But Puskas subsequently denied that he had presented his shirt to anybody.

Later that summer he played for Spain in the World Cup finals in Chile, where he was used in three games at centre-forward. He did not enjoy it, yearning for happier days with Real and Hungary when goals were easier to come by. Spain came last in their group. As Chilean fans later celebrated in the streets after their country's victory in the third-place match, an image remains of Puskas standing alone in a doorway, munching monkey nuts and wearing that Budapest urchin grin which would never desert him.

The following year he returned with distinction to Wembley to play for the Fifa XI which met England, celebrating the 100th anniversary of the Football Association. He came on as a substitute for Eusebio.

Still capable of scoring five goals against Holland's Feyenoord as late as 1965, he retired the following year and went to Canada to coach Vancouver. It was not a positive experience. He was said to have demoralised the club's goalkeepers with the power of his shooting. Subsequently he became manager of Panathinaikos of Athens and got them to Wembley for the European Cup final of 1971, which they lost to Ajax.

After the collapse of communism in eastern Europe, Puskas returned to live in Budapest. In 1999 he was voted the sixth best player of the 20th century, after Pele, Johan Cruyff, Franz Beckenbauer, Alfredo di Stéfano and Diego Maradona. In later years he suffered from Alzheimer's disease. He is survived by his wife, Erzsebet, and a daughter, Aniko.

Ferenc Puskas, born April 2 1927, died November 17 2006

AUGUST 15 2003

Bulldozing winger

HELMUT RAHN

Helmut Rahn, who has died aged 73, was a major force in two World Cups. He scored the winning goal for West Germany in the 1954 final and was the kind of muscular, bulldozing right-winger once famous in British football but now seldom found anywhere.

The remarkable feature of his World Cup games was that he might well have not appeared in them. He was not among the 22 German players chosen for the 1954 series in Switzerland, so went off on tour to South America with his club, Rot Weiss Essen. In Montevideo he played so well against the top Uruguayan club, Peñarol, that they tried to buy him. Sepp Herberger, who had been the German team manager since the 1938 World Cup, heard of his form and summoned him to Switzerland.

Rahn did not figure in the first and third German games but scored in the fiasco of an 8-3 defeat by Hungary. In the quarter-final against Yugoslavia his strong run and finish gave the Germans their second goal four minutes from the end. He failed to score in the semi-final, when Austria were thrashed 6-1 in Basle, but came into his own in the final at Berne.

The general expectation was that the game would be won by Hungary and they duly went into an early 2-0 lead. But the Germans quickly pulled one back through Max Morlock, after Rahn's left-wing cross into the goalmouth, where it took a slight deflection off Hungary's right-half, Jozef Bozsik. Then, after 16 minutes, the Hungarian keeper failed to hold a corner from the German captain Fritz Walter, the ball ran to Rahn and in it went.

It was not with his formidable right foot but his left that Rahn scored the winning goal. An untypical mistake by Bozsik enabled Schaefer to dash away. When the ball flashed across the goal-mouth, it eluded Hungary's left-back Mihaly Lantos, went to Rahn and from 15 yards he won the World Cup for West Germany.

By 1958, when the trophy was due to be defended in Sweden, Rahn had become a heavy drinker, put on weight and been jailed for drink-driving. But Herberger helped his rehabilitation, picked him for the team and was rewarded by another series of inspired performances.

After West Germany went behind to Argentina, Rahn's left foot was evident again when he equalised with a strong shot from an unaccustomed inside-left position. Ten minutes from time he got his team's third goal, showing his technique by bending a shot with the outside of his foot round the Argentinian goalkeeper, Amadeo Carrizo.

In the next group game he scored the equaliser in a hard fought recovery from 0-2 to 2-2 against the Czechs. The score was the same with Northern Ireland, Rahn equalising the first Irish goal. He was then the decisive factor in sustaining the Germans' dominance of the Yugoslavs, scoring the only goal of their quarter-final, though he could not save his team from a 3-1 semi-final defeat by Sweden.

He did, however, score once more – in the meaningless third-place match that saw France's Just Fontaine score four against a weakened West Germany to create a World Cup record of 13 goals. Rahn scored the second German goal in a 6-3 defeat. Even in such company Rahn had proved one of the tournament's most effective forwards.

Born at Alten-Hessen, he first found work as a chauffeur, combining his football with travelling for a confectioner. He won 40 international caps between 1951 and 1960, the first in November 1951 in Istanbul, where West Germany beat Turkey 2-0. His first home appearance for the Germans was at the Rot Weiss Essen ground where he spent the bulk of his career. It came two days before Christmas and Rahn scored in a 4-1 win against Luxembourg.

In total he scored 19 goals for his country, exploiting his pace, power and fearsome right-footed drive. His final goal was in April 1960 against Portugal in Ludwigshafen. He had moved from Essen to Cologne the previous year and also played for the Dutch club Twente Enschede. He later worked as a second-hand car dealer.

His wife, Gerti, and sons, Uwe and Klaus, survive him.

Helmut Rahn, born August 16 1929, died August 14 2003

FEBRUARY 21 2005

Tunnel visionary

OMAR SIVORI

Omar Sivori, who has died aged 69, was one of the finest inside-lefts with one of the finest left feet since the war, an Argentinian player of flair and finishing power who never played for his country in a World Cup but played for Italy instead. A little man who always played with his stockings round his ankles, he gave as good as he got. He later managed Argentina, qualifying them for a World Cup, before returning to Italy to work as a journalist and pungent television commentator.

Born in a suburb of Buenos Aires, he made his name, internationally, in the 1957 South American Championships in Lima. Still only 21, he was one of the so-called Trio of Death with Humberto

Maschio at inside-right and Valentín Angelillo at centre-forward. Rich Italian clubs promptly snapped up all three of them. Sivori went to Juventus, Maschio to Atalanta, Angelillo to Inter Milan. In recent times this would have been no bar to their continuing to play for Argentina. But then Argentina's establishment regarded the three, in footballing terms, as un-persons. They played without them in the 1958 World Cup and were humiliated.

Sivori moved to Juventus from River Plate, the Buenos Aires club, in 1957 for what was then a world record fee of £91,000. At the same time John Charles, the Leeds United centre-forward and Welsh international, also joined the Turin club, for £65,000. Now Sivori found himself in a new inside-forward trio. Its third member was Giampiero Boniperti, who had made his name with Juventus as a centre-forward, had also played for Italy at outside-right but settled in as an inside-right.

That year, 1957-58, Juventus won the Italian Championship, their first for six years, with an eight-point margin over Fiorentina. Sivori figured in 32 of the 34 games, scoring 22 goals. He dove-tailed splendidly with the huge Charles and enraptured the Juve supporters with his so-called 'tunnel', his ability to push the ball between an opponent's legs. Cocky, ebullient, sometimes provocative – when he appeared to be ruffling a fallen opponent's hair, he was sometimes pulling it – he was in character and physique a total contrast to the placid Charles but they complemented one another admirably.

Thanks to their combination, two more Championships followed, in 1960 and 1961. In these, too, Sivori's goalscoring was phenomenal – 27 goals in 31 games and leading Italian championship scorer the first season, 26 in 27 the next.

It was in April 1961 that the Italians, exploiting his Italian descent, as they did with Maschio and Angelillo, capped him for the first time and he scored the winning goal in a 3-2 victory over Northern Ireland. The following month he scored a goal against England in the Olympic Stadium in Rome, spinning on the ball to whip it home with his left foot, though Italy lost the match 3-2. In June he scored twice in a 4-1 victory over Argentina in Florence.

The following November in a World Cup qualifying game in Turin he scored four of Italy's goals in a 6-0 win against Israel. He stayed in the team for the ensuing World Cup finals and played twice in Chile, against West Germany and Switzerland, but was fortunate to miss the so-called Battle of Santiago against Chile, notorious for its violence. In all he made nine appearances for Italy. *Oriundi*, the word given to South Americans of Italian descent, were by then losing favour.

In 1965, having scored 135 championship goals for Juventus, he moved to Napoli but things went awry. Injuries devastated the four seasons he had there and he played only a dozen games, having pocketed a signing-on bonus of £24,000. Alas, badly advised and probably exploited, the money ran out and by the time he went back to Argentina in 1969 there was little left.

As manager of the Argentinian national team his initial impact was dramatic. He took them on a dazzling tour of Europe in 1973, when West Germany were beaten. But by the World Cup finals the next year the volatile Sivori had been dismissed. And in West Germany the team he had left failed sadly.

Omar Sivori, born October 2 1935, died February 17 2005

NOVEMBER 5 2005

Rollercoaster with Italy

FERRUCCIO VALCAREGGI

Ferruccio Valcareggi, who has died aged 86, was a competent inside-forward with a variety of leading Italian clubs, who later became first assistant, then manager of the Italian national team and took them in an eight-year reign to a controversial triumph in the 1968 European Nations' Cup final in Rome.

It was not always a comfortable ride. Even as an assistant manager he was not immune from abuse. This became all too clear in the run-up to Italy's disastrous World Cup finals of 1966. Before a friendly 0-0 draw against France in Paris Valcareggi was grossly insulted by the volatile Inter Milan left-winger, Mariolino Corso. He feigned not to hear the worst of his epithets but the best that could be said for it is that it was some kind of preparation for what followed when he became full manager.

During the 1966 finals Italy were humiliated in Middlesbrough by the North Koreans and it became plain that they would soon be rid of their manager, Edmondo Fabbri. The following season the Italian federation made the odd double appointment of Valcareggi and the flamboyant Helenio Herrera, one-time manager of Barcelona, Inter and Roma. Officially the two men formed the 'technical commission' but Valcareggi was soon given sole charge and they began brightly with a 1-0 win against Romania in Bucharest, a Nations' Cup qualifying game.

Somewhat bumpily Italy made their way to the 1968 final. In the semi-final in Naples they could do no better than draw 0-0 with the Soviet Union. This was before such deadlocks were decided on penalties. Italy prevailed on the toss of a disc.

In the final against Yugoslavia in Rome they survived again, thanks to a scandalous refereeing decision. When the half-back Giorgio Ferrini blatantly charged the Yugoslav attacker, Vahidin Musemic, in the back in the penalty box, Gottfried Dienst, the Swiss referee who had been in charge of the 1966 World Cup final, did nothing. It later transpired that he had been suborned by the notorious match fixer, Italo Allodi, although there is no indication that Valcareggi, a man of integrity, knew anything about that. The Italians drew 1-1 and went on to beat the exhausted Yugoslavs 2-0 in the replay.

Valcareggi then set about qualifying for the 1970 World Cup finals in Mexico. On an experimental tour in January 1969 the *Azzurri*, on the breathless heights of the Azteca stadium in Mexico City, beat Mexico 3-2 and then drew with them, 1-1. The great white hope was Gigi Riva, scoring goal after superb left-footed goal. Qualification was achieved comfortably against Wales and East Germany.

When it came to the finals in Mexico, though, the Italians began uneasily. They beat Sweden 1-0 in Toluca, drew 0-0 with Uruguay in Puebla and drew, goalless again, with modest Israel in Toluca. Things were going wrong, Riva was not scoring, but in the quarter-final against the Mexicans in Toluca, Valcareggi produced his trump card – the so-called *staffetta* or relay, which allowed both his gifted playmakers, Gianni Rivera and Sandrino Mazzola, to play. Rivera, technically so gifted, replaced Mazzola when the score was 1-1 at half-time, inspiring his team to a 4-1 victory, in which he scored himself.

In an eventful semi-final at the Azteca West Germany were beaten 4-3. Again the *staffetta* worked, Rivera coming on at half-time and scoring the winner in extra-time. But the practice backfired in the final, on the same ground, against a dominant Brazil. Mazzola played so splendidly that Rivera got on for only six minutes. Brazil won 4-1.

Valcareggi, however, remained in charge, getting his team to the quarter-finals of the ensuing European Championship. No games were lost against Austria, Ireland and Sweden in the qualifying group but in the quarter-finals Belgium forced a goalless draw in Milan and beat the *Azzurri* 2-1 in Brussels.

Still Valcareggi stayed in office and again he guided his team to the World Cup finals, this time in West Germany in 1974. No group games were lost against Luxembourg, Switzerland and Turkey, although the Turks drew 0-0 in Naples. But with Italo Allodi controversially made general manager for the finals, things began to go wrong.

The first match, against Haiti in Munich, almost became a painful embarrassment as Italy fell behind to a 46th-minute goal. When the big centre-forward Giorgio Chinaglia was substituted in the second half, he insulted Valcareggi as he strode past the dug-out, went into the dressing room and smashed an array of mineral water bottles. In the end the *Azzurri* won the game 3-1.

In Stuttgart, against Argentina, Italy got their initial tactics wildly wrong, though this was the fault largely of Valcareggi's coach. A goal down, they eventually drew 1-1 but the Poles then knocked them out 2-1 on the same ground amid rumours that the Italians had tried to bribe them. Again Valcareggi was in no way impugned. He was, however, replaced as manager by Fulvio Bernardini.

At a time when the exciting total football was being played by the Germans and Dutch Valcareggi stuck to the old, cautious methods of *catenaccio*, with its sweeper playing behind two markers, but he did not discourage enterprise. He was a decent, kindly man who did his best under enormous pressure. Leaving the Italian job, he became manager of Verona.

Born in Trieste, he played as an inside-right for his local club, Triestina, then for Fiorentina, whom he joined in 1940, Bologna, Fiorentina again, Vicenza and Lucchese. In 1944 he played for Milan in the wartime Lombardy regional league. He began as a coach with Prato before moving on to Atalanta and Fiorentina. Then came the national team.

He is survived by his wife and son.

Ferruccio Valcareggi, born February 12 1919, died November 2 2005

JUNE 18 2002

Manager on the field

FRITZ WALTER

For more than a decade of the post-war years Fritz Walter, who has died aged 81, was the standard bearer of West German football. An inside-forward, first renowned as a goalscorer, latterly as a creative influence, he was a captain of weight and influence who led his national team to the 1954 World Cup in Switzerland, enabling Germans to say, 'We're somebody again.' Four years later he took them to the semi-final in Sweden. It is said that, though Walter retired a couple of years later, the manager Sepp Herberger tried to persuade him to play in the Chilean World Cup final of 1962.

Walter spent the whole of his footballing career with his local club Kaiserslautern and remained in the town after retirement running, at various times, with his Italian-born wife Italia, a cinema and a laundrette. At the end of the war he had a season in charge of Kaiserslautern. On retirement he had a three-year, highly successful spell with a nearby club, SV Alsenborn.

His 18-year-long international career began as a centre-forward in 1940, against Romania. Germany, which carried on full internationals for several years of the war, won 9-3, Walter scoring a hat-trick. Well-built, forceful yet technically adroit, and an excellent passer, he kept his place in the team.

All in all he would play 61 times for Germany, scoring 33 goals. By the time the international team stopped, after a 5-2 win against Slovakia, Walter, still chiefly a centre-forward (as his younger brother Otmar would become), had missed only a couple of games and scored another 19 goals. He then joined the paratroop corps and, so the story goes, was so traumatised when he saw a fellow soldier killed as he was about to jump that he refused to fly again after the war.

When the West German team began international play in November 1950, after a four-year Fifa ban, it was Otmar who won his first cap at centre-forward; Fritz did not play. Both, though, were in the team the following autumn, when Germany beat Switzerland 3-2 in Zurich. Both Walters scored – a prelude to their success three years later – and Fritz captained West Germany for the first time. He held that position until he dropped out of the team after playing in a 3-1 defeat by Sweden in November 1956.

When he returned in March 1958, Hans Schaefer was captain, a role he continued to fill throughout the 1958 World Cup finals, although Walter remained beyond doubt the team's dominant personality. Indeed, in October 1955, a French magazine published a surprising statement by a German critic: 'The Yugoslavs,' he wrote, 'have called the German side "a team without imagination". I fear they may be right. Isn't it to a lack of imagination, the regrettable *führer* principle, that too many Germans pay homage? Fritz Walter is certainly the greatest German footballer of our

generation and, even if you take account of the fact that he will
turn 35 this month, he is still a remarkable inspiration. But they
play too much for him.'

That was somewhat harsh on Walter, perhaps, since the real
führer of the German team was surely Herberger, who had taken
over in 1938 and would remain there until after the 1962 World
Cup. At most Walter could be designated what Italians call 'the
manager on the field'.

When West Germany arrived in Switzerland for the 1954 World
Cup finals, few gave them any chance. True, they had qualified
without difficulty and had beaten Switzerland 5-3 the previous
April, with Walter, at inside-left, scoring two goals. Nor had they
been beaten since October 1952, when they lost 3-1 to France. But
Hungary were the hot favourites. And when the teams met in the
Germans' second group game, Hungary triumphed 8-3.

Next time out, though, in a play-off, a stronger German team
annihilated Turkey 7-2, having already beaten them 4-1 in their
initial match. The Walter brothers scored a goal each. But when
Yugoslavia became their quarter-final opponents, few fancied the
Germans. Indeed, they were outplayed for much of the game and
cleared several shots off the line. But an own-goal by Ivan Horvat
and a shot from the powerful right-winger Helmut Rahn put the
Germans into the semi-finals.

Here, once more, they were seen as the underdogs to a gifted
Austrian team. Instead the Austrians were overrun. Walter pulled
the strings to formidable effect. Four of the Germans' half-dozen
goals came from set pieces and he coolly scored twice from the
penalty spot. After the first 20 minutes, when the Austrians
seemed comfortably in command, Max Morlock, the German
inside-right, sent Walter away on the right flank. A precise cross
reached Hans Schaefer, who flicked it into the goal. The second
half was a German holiday. In the third minute a well-placed

corner by Walter made the second goal. The fourth was scored from another of his corners by his brother, Otmar. With both his penalties he sent Walter Zeman the wrong way. For the sixth German goal in this 6-1 victory he sent Schaefer down the left for Otmar to head in the centre.

So to the final, with West Germany yet again the underdogs. When the Hungarians went 2-0 ahead after eight minutes, it seemed that, at last, the Germans had been found out. Not a bit of it. Though they created perhaps half a dozen chances in the game, they exploited three of them. Three minutes after the second Hungarian goal Rahn sent in a fast cross, Morlock got a foot to it and the score was 2-1. Walter was involved in Germany's late winner. His centre was only half cleared and Rahn, who had scored the equaliser from a Walter corner, shot past Gyula Grosics from 15 yards.

The 1958 World Cup saw Walter operating at inside-right. In the semi-final West Germany went down 3-1 to the home team, Sweden, and Walter was badly hurt by Sigge Parling. In time Helmut Schoen would build a more elegant, technical German team, inspired by Franz Beckenbauer. But he was no more inspirational than Fritz Walter.

Fritz Walter, born October 31 1920, died June 17 2002

8

Managers Last
and Foremost

Soul of the Saints

TED BATES

Ted Bates, who has died aged 85, might be seen as the very soul of Southampton Football Club. At various times he was their accomplished inside-right, manager, chief executive, director and president. Altogether his career there spanned an astonishing 66 years.

Bates's longevity as manager, from 1955 to 1973, would be inconceivable in today's frantic times. Well might the current Southampton chairman, Rupert Lowe, declare that he 'epitomised what the club is all about with his decency and dignity, his loyalty, ability and his experience'.

A Norfolk man, born in Thetford, Bates joined the Saints as a player in 1937 and played 216 competitive games for them, scoring 64 goals, many of them with his head since, though he was no giant, standing little more than 5ft 8in tall and weighing 11st, his leaps could be prodigious. A newspaper report of a mid-1940s match at White Hart Lane referred to 'the ostrich-necked Bates'.

Though it would not be until 1966 that Southampton first attained the top division, he and his team all but achieved that promotion as long before as the 1948-49 season, when he was still playing, and would surely have done so had Charlie Wayman, their elusive and prolific centre-forward not been injured. Having scored 32 Second Division goals, Wayman missed the last seven league games. Southampton took a mere four points to finish third for the second season in succession, a point short of second.

Always pleasant, humorous and relaxed, whatever the pressures, Bates – whose real first name was Edric – was a fount of good sense. Apropos of the competitive influence on young footballers, he once said: 'They learn to win before they can play.'

At the start of the Second World War Bates initially worked for Folland Aircraft, then joined the police war reserve and finally went into the army. Back at The Dell he enjoyed a fine wing partnership with Don Roper, a highly effective outside-right, until Arsenal bought the latter in the summer of 1947.

Bates was appointed Southampton's coach in 1953, moving up to manager in 1955. In those years the club, never one of the game's richest, had its ups and downs – relegated from the Second Division in 1953, promoted back in 1960. Meanwhile Bates launched such talent as Terry Paine, the Hampshire man who shone for years on the Southampton right wing and was often capped by England. Later he gave a break to another outstanding, home-grown attacker and England international in Mike Channon, a star of the 1970s and later a successful racehorse trainer. As manager Bates also appointed his wife, Mary, as club secretary. Southampton was truly a family club.

Apart from nurturing young talent Bates dealt shrewdly in the transfer market, seldom more so than when he paid £55,000 for the Welsh international centre-forward Ron Davies, whose goals did much to win that promotion to the First Division.

On retiring as manager Bates became chief executive in 1973, was made a director in 1978, vice-president in 1993 and president in 1998. In 2001 he was awarded the MBE and received the freedom of the City of Southampton. He is survived by Mary and two daughters.

Edric 'Ted' Bates, born May 3 1918, died November 26 2003

Maverick force

BRIAN CLOUGH

A prolific but unlucky centre-forward, who became a triumphant but star-crossed manager, Brian Clough, who has died of stomach cancer aged 69, was, in some sense, the victim of his own public image. He was a mixture of arrogance and initiative, bombast and generosity, intransigence and self-doubt.

He scored 197 Second Division goals in 213 games for Middlesbrough, an astonishing strike rate matched by 54 in 61 for Sunderland, yet won only a couple of England caps, against Wales and Sweden in 1959. As a manager he transformed Derby County into a Championship-winning team, won the European Cup twice with Nottingham Forest, yet failed both at Brighton and Leeds and never achieved the managership of England he coveted.

Through almost the whole of Clough's career runs the theme of his collaboration with Peter Taylor. When Clough went back to his local club, Middlesbrough, after RAF service, he was scarcely a third-choice centre-forward. It was Taylor, a reserve goalkeeper, who saw his potential, trumpeted his virtues and promoted his career, with Clough's league debut coming against Barnsley in 1955.

When that career came to a bitter end on Boxing Day 1962, playing for Sunderland, for whom he had signed in 1961, it was with Taylor that Clough began his remarkable career in management. He was only 27 when a collision with Bury's goalkeeper tore a cruciate ligament beyond repair. When George Hardwick, another former Middlesbrough player and an ex-England captain, made him youth coach, Clough's misery was partly assuaged. But the directors would not have him. He was dismissed, drank heavily, despaired and found himself, in 1965, manager of nearby Hartlepools United. Taylor left his job as Burton Albion manager to assist him.

Between them the two men breathed life into a club forever on the verge of extinction and, in 1967, they were appointed to run Derby, then in the Second Division. Showing enormous flair in the transfer market – acquiring for small fees such future stars as Roy McFarland and Archie Gemmill – the two transformed Derby as well. In 1972 they won the Championship but their relationship even then was showing signs of strain. It steadily deteriorated over the years until, like some impossible marriage, it degenerated into implacable hostility, still unresolved at the time of Taylor's death in 1990.

Taylor was enraged when he found Clough had been given a £5,000 salary increase without telling him and things would never be the same. In October 1973, after Clough had taken Derby to the semi-finals of the European Cup, he and a competitive chairman, Sam Longson, fell out irreparably, Clough and Taylor resigned and, despite impassioned protest meetings in the town, would not find a way back. Years later, in 1982, Taylor alone returned to the Baseball Ground as manager and clashed violently with Clough again when he signed Nottingham Forest's outside-left, John Robertson, without telling him.

The two of them revolutionised Forest as they had Derby but not before they had utterly failed, from November 1973, to do the same for the Third Division club Brighton and Hove Albion, where Clough's attempt to bully limited players to perform like stars brought disastrous results. Surprisingly, in July 1974, he was engaged to manage Leeds United, whose players he had publicly condemned as cheats in the past and who fully reciprocated his antagonism. Clough lasted 44 days and emerged a demoralised man.

However, in January 1975 he became manager of Derby's eternal rivals, Nottingham Forest, and in the summer of 1976 Taylor, having resigned as manager of Brighton, joined him. Only then did things begin to move. Showing their old flair for signing players, they took Forest out of the Second Division in 1977, won the Championship in 1978 and the European Cup in 1979 and 1980.

This was an astonishing achievement with a club that had won nothing of consequence since the FA Cup in 1959. That particular domestic trophy eluded Clough – Tottenham beat Forest in the 1991 final – but League Cup victories came in 1978, 1979, 1989 and 1990.

Clough's methods were unique. He was essentially a dictator and not always a benevolent one. 'Have you ever been punched in the stomach, young man?' he once asked a centre-forward, Nigel Jemson, in the dressing room. When the answer was no, Clough suited the action to the word, remarking, 'Well, now you have.'

After Forest supporters invaded the pitch at the end of a tumultuous League Cup quarter-final victory over Queens Park Rangers in February 1989, Clough took the field himself and clipped several fans in ancient schoolmasterly fashion. He was fined £5,000 for bringing the game into disrepute and banned from the touchline of all Football League grounds for the rest of the season.

When Everton's players, disappointed by losing a League Cup match to a controversial goal, despoiled their dressing room, Clough told the cleaners to leave it as it was. He knew Everton were back again for a league match three days later. They duly found it as they left it. After Derby had lost a European Cup semi-final game against Juventus in Turin in April 1973, Clough emerged from the dressing room and told expectant Italian reporters: 'I will not talk to any cheating bastards.' Having shut the dressing-room door, he re-emerged to say to myself: 'Tell them what I said Brian.'

Clough was born in Middlesbrough, the sixth of nine children, of whom the first, a girl, had died at the age of four. His father, Joe, wounded in the First World War, worked at various times for nearby ICI and in a sweet factory. His resilient mother, Sally, was extremely close to him and was reportedly 'fanatical' about football.

In later years Clough was a professed socialist, once parking his Mercedes outside a church hall in Nottingham before giving an emotional speech supporting the Labour candidate in the 1979 election, Phillip Whitehead.

Clough married Barbara Glasgow, a neighbour, while still playing for Middlesbrough. Of their three children, Simon, Nigel and Libby, it was Nigel who followed his father into football. A boisterous child who developed into a quiet, calm young man and a gifted centre-forward in a far less robust and more inventive style than his father's, he was long the fulcrum of the Forest attack before joining Liverpool, then Manchester City.

Clough Sr, not often to be found at the training pitch but always influential when he was there, was given to late, inspirational appearances in pre-match dressing-rooms. On April 26 1993, though, at 58, he finally retired. The team faced relegation and he himself no longer had the same resilient hubris. He had been in charge of Forest for 18 years and worked wonders at the City Ground.

In January 2003 his years of heavy drinking caught up with him and he was obliged to undergo a liver transplant in a 10-hour operation carried out in Newcastle. Doctors had told him that without it he had only a few months to live. Clough said he was persuaded to have the operation when his grandson Stephen begged him to stop drinking. 'Drink,' Clough admitted, 'became more important to me than the anguish I was creating for those I loved most.' His wife and children survive him.

Brian Clough, born March 21 1935, died September 20 2004

MARCH 1 2001

Flipper the skipper

STAN CULLIS

Stan Cullis, who has died aged 84, managed Wolverhampton Wanderers during the club's European glory days in the 1950s and steered them to three League titles. He was also one of the finest centre-halves of his day and a former England captain.

Cullis was born in Ellesmere Port, Cheshire, but his father was a Wolverhampton man and Wolves could thank Cullis Sr for Stanley going to Molineux. Several major clubs had shown interest in him when he was playing as a teenager for Ellesmere Port but his father, wanting to get him to Wolves, wrote to recommend him. They signed him up in 1934, after a trial, and he became skipper of the A team at 17, the reserves at 18 and the first team by the time he was 19. An especially notable month for him was May 1939 when, in Bucharest against Romania, he was made captain of the England team, the youngest ever at 22. England won 2-0.

Wolves were known then as the Buckley Babes, after their flamboyant manager, Major Frank Buckley. His emphasis was very much on youth. He had fielded the 16-year-old outside-left, Jimmy Mullen, later to become an English international of renown, in the FA Cup semi-final of 1939. The team, moreover, were supposed to derive their pace and energy from monkey glands, though this may be the stuff of legend.

At all events they were red-hot favourites to win the final at Wembley, against a seemingly workaday Portsmouth. But when the book which players were expected to sign before the game was brought from the Wolves dressing-room into Portsmouth's, the

Pompey players suddenly reckoned they were on to a good thing. The Wolves' signatures were shaky and illegible. Portsmouth won at a canter, 4-1.

Salt may have been rubbed into Cullis's wounds. By tradition Madame Tussauds customarily featured models of the two captains shaking hands before the game. Usually the models would be in place for only a year but, since 'official' football was abandoned in 1939, the loser Cullis and Portsmouth's Jimmy Guthrie remained their waxwork selves until after the FA Cup final of 1946.

In the era of the third-back game and the stopper centre-half Cullis was sometimes misnamed an attacking centre-half, a figure which had long disappeared from British football. But he was certainly a footballing centre-half. Though strong in the tackle and capable in the air, he was skilful and composed on the ball. The sight of him coolly holding off the challenge of several Scottish forwards when playing for England at Wembley on a snow-covered pitch in January 1942 was not easily forgotten.

He was polished rather than elegant. His arms-akimbo style led his fellow England players to nickname him Flipper. But he had their deep respect, not least throughout the war, when he was the centre of a famous half-back line, with the two Everton players Cliff Britton and Joe Mercer on either side of him. His use of the ball, besides, was always shrewd. All three players, like so many professional footballers, were drafted into the Army Physical Training Corps. This meant being based at Aldershot, and the local Third Division club could thus field the England half-back line in its entirety as 'guest' players.

Cullis, who never lost his Black Country accent, would have won many more than his 12 international caps had wartime internationals been officially recognised. Eddie Hapgood of Arsenal, a celebrated captain of England himself, picked Cullis in his best-ever team, calling him 'an intelligent, defensive centre-half who varied his play by attacking when the situation warranted this method. Stanley has mannerisms which sometimes annoy onlookers but nothing ruffles him. He goes his own way, thoughtfully, always looking for the opportunity of a crack down the middle.'

Hapgood also told the tale of how Cullis surprised the other England players on tour in Europe, after they had been teasing him about his study of foreign languages. Always a great one for self-improvement, a night-school man, Cullis was known to have applied himself to Esperanto and to French. An England player who had been foremost in the taunting challenged Cullis to ask a Frenchman for directions. Far from being discomfited, Cullis conversed with the man in fluent French.

His playing career came to a disappointingly early end, for those who admired him. Serving with the army in Europe, he inevitably lost fitness and returned early in 1946 for an embarrassing game for Wolves against Arsenal at Tottenham, so short of pace that he was most untypically reduced to grabbing his opposing centre-forward, Reg Lewis, by the shirt, to the scorn of the crowd.

He recovered form to captain Wolves with flair and authority in the first post-war official season, 1946-47, which began with a 6-1 win against Arsenal. Wolves seemed odds on for the Championship but an appalling winter with endless cancellations extended the season well into the summer. Wolves faltered on the harder going and lost their last match at home to Liverpool and with it the title to their opponents.

So, at only 31, and after 152 league games for Wolves, Cullis retired to become assistant manager, then in 1948 manager itself. He proved a highly motivated and successful one, though his tactics did not endear him and his team to everyone. He was a powerful, authoritarian figure. Most of his players would have died for him but others, youngsters especially, later complained that he had treated them harshly.

Wolves' methods were deeply influenced by the theories of Charles Reep, a retired RAF wing commander, who had worked as an accountant. In those pre-computer days Reep's elaborate theories of match analysis were expounded in the old *News Chronicle* in an infinity of squiggly diagrams. The essence of the theory was that the ball should be propelled into the danger zones as quickly as possible, ideally with long passes. So the premium was on pace and power, rather than ball play and an elaborate build-up.

'Flying wingers' were the essence of Wolves' game and Cullis had them *par excellence* in the now mature Mullen on the left and little Johnny Hancocks, bought cheaply from nearby Walsall, on the right. They poured their centres into the penalty box where such attackers as Jesse Pye, bought from Notts County as an inside-right but converted to centre-forward, exploited them with foot or head.

Sitting in the press box in front of Cullis in the directors' box – managers did not then shout and scream from the dug-out – could be a revealing experience. 'Tip-tap, tip-tap,' he would say acidly when the passes were not long enough for him, to be followed by a satisfied 'thump-thump, thump-thump' when the long balls started going in.

However controversial the style, there was no denying its consistent success. And the superb individual goal which the red-haired Irish international inside-forward Sammy Smyth scored for Wolves when they beat Leicester 3-1 in the 1949 Cup final would have graced any team.

Cullis had the ideal adjutant in his and England's captain, Billy Wright, a blond wing-half of boyish enthusiasm who later in his career became a fine centre-half and was always, like Cullis himself, a Wolves player.

Famous floodlit victories were won at Molineux against Hungary's then formidable Honved (3-2), despite the presence of six of the Hungarians who had humbled England 6-3 at Wembley in 1953, Moscow Dynamo (2-1) and Moscow Spartak (4-0). Wolves won the League Championship in 1954, 1958 and 1959, finished runners-up in 1950, 1955 and 1960, and came third in 1953 and 1956. They also lifted the FA Cup in 1949 and in 1960, though Blackburn, their victims, were reduced to 10 men. In the dressing room afterwards Cullis showed a humorous side in lamenting that the cup was a nuisance: "You have to take it to this flopping fete and that flopping fete." He never swore.

In Europe, however, Wolves' style was much less effective and there were two memorable thrashings by a polyglot Barcelona – one, in the mud of Molineux, when five goals were conceded.

Wolves slid away in those early 60s, living in the shadow of Manchester United and Matt Busby. In September 1964 they dropped the pilot. Cullis was rather shabbily dismissed and Wolves have never really been the same since.

After vowing not to return to football and spurning a big offer from Juventus Cullis re-emerged as manager of Birmingham City a year later but somehow the virtue seemed to have gone out of him and he could not conjure up the same success. After leaving Birmingham in 1970 he worked in a photography business. In 1992 Wolves and Aston Villa played a testimonial match for him and there are plans for a statue outside Molineux.

His wife, Winifred, predeceased him and he is survived by his son, Andrew, who became a vicar, and daughter, Susan.

Stanley Cullis, born October 25 1916, died February 27 2001

AUGUST 16 2000

Cockney quintessence

BENNY FENTON

The footballer and manager Benny Fenton, who has died aged 81, was the quintessence of cockneyism. Born in West Ham, he began his career with that club like his older brother Ted but, whereas Ted, a centre-half, stayed at Upton Park, Benny would migrate, though never far from home.

Initially an inside-right, at times a centre-forward, with quick responses and good feet, he moved to Millwall and, in January 1947, to Charlton Athletic, a top-division club. He was signed too late to figure in the ensuing FA Cup final, which Charlton won, but went on to play in 264 games, scoring 54 goals for the club. He had successfully converted to right-half and, a wily player rather than a hard one, was known for the innocence of his expression when typically stealing ground at a throw-in.

In the 1950-51 season Fenton was made Charlton's captain which, said a contemporary account, 'sobered and improved his play immensely. An inspiration to his team.' On retirement he became, like Ted, a manager and both of them in their turn took charge of Colchester United. Ted led them as a player-manager on a celebrated FA Cup run, when they were still a non-league side in 1947-48; Benny managed them between 1955 and 1963.

But Benny Fenton's best years in management were at Millwall, between 1966 and 1974. Billy Gray, his predecessor, aided by his coach, Bill Dodgin Jr, had weaned the team on to a more technical, progressive game and Fenton continued in this vein, though his ducking and diving under any kind of pressure became a byword.

There was, for example, the notorious Saturday afternoon when Millwall fans invaded the pitch and the referee was punched in the stomach. Ground closure loomed, by no means for the first time, and Fenton had to be very quick on his feet. 'Punched in the stomach?' he said. 'Never.' Which raised the interesting possibility, as was said at the time, that the punch was self-inflicted.

Millwall, when Fenton took over, was still the only London club never to be promoted to the top division and he could not quite get them there himself. In 1972 a single point divided them from Birmingham City, who beat them at St Andrew's in a crucial game. The very word 'promotion' had been taboo to Fenton and at the mention of it he reacted like a vampire confronted by a wreath of garlic.

Eamonn Dunphy's celebrated diary, *Only a Game*, the product of his days as a creative inside-forward, somewhat lampoons Fenton but Dennis Burnett, a defender, once persuaded to play with a burst blood vessel, called him 'a good manager of men' while his centre-forward, Barry Bridges, an ex-England player, said: 'I've never seen a bunch of lads who put everything into their training as much as these. Benny's doing it all himself and he's doing a hell of a good job. He wants everybody to look the part. Before you go out for the game, everything's got to be right, shorts have got to be pulled up, socks have got to be straight.'

Alas, when it came to that Birmingham game, Fenton's nerve failed him. He played an ultra-defensive system and lost to what seemed an offside goal.

He was, nonetheless, a beguiling raconteur. One remembers especially a tale he told about Leslie Welch, the 'memory man' who answered an infinity of sports queries on radio and in the music halls. 'Me and Ted are down at Southend, walking along the promenade, when who do we meet? Leslie Welch. He says, "Hello lads, lovely to see you. I'm in a show down here; there's a couple of tickets. And lads, do me a favour. When I come on tonight, ask me this question!"

'And he gives it to us. So we're sitting there, Leslie comes on, Ted asks the question and you know what he says? He says: "Would you mind repeating that?"'

Benny Fenton's later years were spent, in various capacities, with Charlton. He latterly lived in Dorset and is survived by his wife, Winnie, whom he married on Christmas Day 1939, their daughter, two grandchildren and one great grandchild.

Benny Fenton, born October 28 1918, died July 29 2000

FEBRUARY 10 2006

Purist made for West Ham

RON GREENWOOD

When Ron Greenwood, who has died aged 84, worked as a teenager on the ground staff at Wembley Stadium before the Second World War he could hardly have expected to return there as England's team manager. But he did. In 1977, when Don Revie abruptly deserted the position, the Oxford don Sir Harold Thompson, chairman of the Football Association, looking for an equivalent of the white hen that never laid a stray egg, turned to the retired Greenwood, who then stayed in the post until 1982.

Before that Greenwood had been, from 1961 to 1977, manager, coach and general manager of West Ham United. There were FA Cups in 1964 and 1975 (when John Lyall was manager) and the European Cup-Winners' Cup in 1965, when West Ham beat Munich 1860. Under Greenwood's shrewd, perfectionist rule West Ham became the crucible of skilful football. Oddly he probably did more for the England team that won the 1966 World Cup by helping the development of Bobby Moore, Geoff Hurst and Martin Peters than he did as manager in the 1982 World Cup in Spain.

Though born in Burnley, Greenwood grew up and was educated in Alperton, north-west London. He showed precocious footballing promise, playing inside-left for the district school side when he was only eight. He became an apprentice sign writer in 1937 but his skill in minor football circles in the Wembley area was spotted and in 1940 he was signed by Chelsea, the club with which, in the 1954-55 season, he won a League Championship medal.

But also in 1940 war saw him begin five years in the RAF. In December 1945 Chelsea pocketed a large fee when they sold Greenwood, by now a solidly built, strong-tackling centre-half, to the Second Division Bradford Park Avenue, where he was captain. In 1948-49 Bradford themselves got a substantial sum by transferring him to Brentford, for whom he played more than 300 matches.

Chelsea bought him back in 1952 and in the 1954-55 season he made 21 appearances, half the total, in an era when they won what would, until the 21st century, be their only Championship. Greenwood moved on to Fulham in 1955, where he ended an honourable, if not exceptional, playing career.

He had long been interested in coaching, held a full FA coaching badge and coached the Oxford University team for three years, a crucial factor when he became England manager largely because Thompson, the dominating figure in Oxford football, had become equally powerful at the FA. In the mid-1950s Greenwood coached the Arsenal team – he was assistant manager in 1958 under George Swindin, though their philosophies were very different. Greenwood was essentially a purist who believed in the arts and skills of the game. He was also an idealist, which accounted largely for his resignation as West Ham's team manager much later. He was distressed by the way the professional game was going.

He had a spell managing amateur Eastbourne United and the England youth team but the watershed of his career came when he was appointed manager of West Ham. 'The crowds at West Ham haven't been rewarded by results,' he observed in 1977, 'but they keep turning up because of the good football they see. Other clubs will suffer from the old bugbear that results count more than anything. This has been the ruination of English soccer.' Greenwood was being hard on himself. Under his aegis West Ham had had their triumphs.

Certainly, too, Moore, Hurst and Peters all owed much to him. Moore was initially a centre-back, not especially strong in the air and certainly not quick. When Greenwood transformed him into a second stopper, playing on the left of the centre-half, he emerged as an outstanding defender, a regular England player at 21 and outstanding captain in the 1966 and 1970 World Cup tournaments.

Of Peters, who came into the England team during the 1966 tournament, it was said he was 10 years ahead of his time. Hurst was a workaday wing-half whom Greenwood almost transferred to Southend United. Then he changed his mind, turned him into a striker and Hurst went on to score a hat-trick in the 1966 World Cup final.

Always didactic, Greenwood used to emphasise what he called 'good habits' – the ones that benefited not only the World Cup three but successors like Trevor Brooking. Whether it was wise to make him England manager is a moot point. He seemed to have retired not only in body but in spirit, disillusioned with the game and curiously unfaithful to his protégés. For example he left Brooking out of a Wembley international, preferring a clutch of less gifted Liverpool players. Later, after the talented Glenn Hoddle crowned a fine debut for England against Bulgaria with a spectacular goal,

Greenwood dropped him with the remark that 'disappointment is part of football'. By contrast he seemed over indulgent to a Kevin Keegan plainly no longer the force he once was.

Greenwood memorably remarked in 1978 that 'football is a simple game. The hard part is making it look simple.' His autobiography, *Yours Sincerely*, appeared in 1984. He is survived by his wife, Lucy, and his son and daughter.

Ronald Greenwood, born November 11 1921, died February 9 2006

OCTOBER 25 2004

Play it down, keep it simple

BILL NICHOLSON

When Bill Nicholson, who has died aged 85, was made manager of Tottenham Hotspur in 1958, the club he had joined as a player before the Second World War and then served as a coach, he scarcely believed it. He did not even tell his loyal and long-suffering wife, Grace, always known as Darkie, who found out about it second hand. Though an ardent Spurs fan, she was, in any case, banned by him from attending any matches for reasons of superstition, as were his daughters, Jean and Linda.

Yet in Nicholson's first five years in the post Spurs won the Championship and the FA Cup in 1961 – the century's first instance of that double – the FA Cup again in 1962 and the European Cup-Winners' Cup in 1963. In an age of flashy club managers, forever rattling their jewellery, Nicholson remained the same taciturn and modest Yorkshireman he had been when he joined the club in 1936. The key to his character was perhaps that, having been brought up in a large family in Scarborough during the Depression, he expected and demanded little out of life and was surprised by what he eventually got.

His father was a groom in the winter and drove a horse-drawn cab along the sea front in the summer. Bill was the only one of the five sons and four daughters to gain a scholarship to Scarborough High School. On leaving he worked in a laundry. However, a happy chance led a local dentist, who ran the Young Liberals team that Nicholson played for, to recommend him to Spurs, who took him on as a ground-staff boy.

Gingery-haired and compactly built, he was an inside-left at first and played stopper and full-back, too. After a war throughout which he was a sergeant physical education instructor in the Durham Light Infantry, he settled down as a right-half.

Typically provident, he lost no time on leaving the army in qualifying as an FA coach. Coaching, indeed, would always be his forte. Perhaps the most famous example of it was in the 1958 World Cup in Gothenburg. Working as assistant to England's team manager, Walter Winterbottom, Nicholson devised a strategy whereby England were able to hold Brazil, the eventual World Cup winners, to a goalless draw. His coaching method consisted largely in isolating a weakness and concentrating on eliminating it.

In 1949 Arthur Rowe, once Tottenham's centre-half, arrived as manager, initiating the classic push-and-run style. Nicholson played in front of the new right-back, Alf Ramsey, and, the sceptics would say, 'did his tackling for him'. Nicholson was a bread-and-butter player but a vital one. He had much to do with Tottenham's successive titles in the Second and First Divisions in 1950 and 1951. In May 1951 he was capped for England against Portugal at Everton and scored one of his rare goals within 19 seconds. The next autumn he was chosen to play against Austria at Wembley, the plan being that Billy Wright, the right-half and captain, would operate at inside-left, marking Austria's Ernst Ocwirk, but Nicholson was injured. He never got another chance.

While still playing he coached Cambridge University and enjoyed it, though well aware that a football brain and an academic brain were two different things. 'I prefer players not to be too good or clever at other things,' he observed. This inevitably caused potential problems when the captain of his double-winning team was Danny Blanchflower. The loquacious Ulsterman was a right-half like 'Billy Nick' but there the resemblance ended. Where Nicholson was fustian, Blanchflower was all flair and illumination, a tremendous inspiration to his teams. Occasional clashes were inevitable but overall they complemented one another and the partnership worked remarkably well.

There was a celebrated occasion when, in Rotterdam, Spurs met Atlético Madrid in the 1963 final of the Cup-Winners' Cup. Thorough and typically glum, Nicholson gave his tactical talk, extolling the merits of the various Atlético players to such an extent that Blanchflower saw the heads going down. He followed up, therefore, with a team talk of his own, extolling the virtues of the Tottenham players. Heads went up and Tottenham won 5-1 at a canter.

An outstanding coach who always knew what he wanted from his players, Nicholson was an almost instant success once he had recovered from the shock of the chairman telling him he would now be the manager. But he continued, unlike most managers, to change in the players' dressing-room and to live in the same modest house he had been given as a player.

He skilfully used the secretarial office next to his own as a sounding board but man management was not his strong point. Once, when Spurs' big, but elegant, centre-forward Martin Chivers had scored goals in an important game, Nicholson said: 'I told him afterwards that was a sitter that he missed. And then I thought, maybe I should have said, "well played" and then told him.'

Nicholson lasted as manager longer than most, not least perhaps because his job obsessed him. He was in tears at the wedding of one of his daughters, remarking that he had not 'seen her grow up'. Spurs won another European trophy, the Uefa Cup, in 1972, to add to a third FA Cup in 1967 and the League Cup in 1971 and 1973. But things went awry in the 1974-75 season. Nicholson resigned and worked for West Ham but returned to Spurs as a consultant from 1976 to 1991, when he was named president. The club now display a bust of their most successful manager. His wife and daughters survive him.

Bill Nicholson, born January 26 1919, died October 23 2004

MAY 1 1999

Grocer to General

SIR ALF RAMSEY

Sir Alf Ramsey, distinguished footballer and still more distinguished manager, who took England to their only World Cup final victory in 1966 at Wembley, has died aged 79. Though he would win so many honours as player and manager, he came curiously late to the game, turning professional with Southampton only when he was 24.

Born in Dagenham, Essex, later an East End overspill town, he originally intended to become a grocer and unfair analogies might be drawn with 'Grocer' Heath since, like the former prime minister,

Ramsey worked with limited success on his accent. But it never prevented him from getting through to the players he initially managed, with success almost unlimited.

Joining the army – the Duke of Cornwall's Light Infantry – in 1940 proved the turning point in his life. Southampton noted him when he played for his battalion against them. Southampton won the game 10-0 but Ramsey had impressed them enough to be signed on amateur forms. He was then a centre-forward with a powerful right-footed shot but after he finally turned professional in 1944 Bill Dodgin Sr, the club's first post-war manager, switched him to right-back.

Impressed by the poise of the Manchester City left-back Sam Barkas and encouraged to practise by the former Portsmouth left-back Bill Rochford, Ramsey won his first England cap in December 1948 against Switzerland at Highbury, only to lose his place for both club and country the following year to Bill Ellerington.

Southampton's loss was Tottenham's gain. Arthur Rowe signed Ramsey in the summer of 1949 and he became the most influential player in Tottenham's push-and-run side which won the Second, then First Division in successive seasons. Nicknamed 'the general', he was a calming and reassuring influence on the whole team. He had little pace and was much assisted by his right-half, Bill Nicholson, and his outside-right, Sonny Walter. But his positional sense was excellent; he always used the ball with skill and his passes back to the goalkeeper, Ted Ditchburn, often broke up one attack and set off another. Such back passes, however, had their dangers, notably in 1951 when one cost a crucial goal in an FA Cup semi-final at Villa Park against Blackpool.

Ramsey next played for England in the 1950 World Cup series in Brazil, including the ill-fated game at Belo Horizonte when they lost 1-0 to the United States. Altogether he gained 32 England caps.

In 1955 he became manager of the then unfashionable Third

Division South side, Ipswich Town. Cleverly making the most of scant resources, using the fragile Scots veteran Jimmy Leadbetter as a deep left-winger to supply a forceful spearhead of Ted Phillips and Ray Crawford, Ramsey got Ipswich promotion in his second season. In 1961 they topped the Second Division and, echoing Tottenham's achievement a decade earlier, took the Championship in 1962.

Ramsey was loyally supported by the patrician Cobbold family, who owned the club. There could scarcely have been a greater contrast between him and the racily uninhibited chairman, John Cobbold, but the two men complemented each other admirably. That year Ramsey also took over as manager of the England team, knowing that his country would host the World Cup finals in 1966. Uncharacteristically he announced that England would win the World Cup. Things started badly when, early the following year, they lost 5-2 to France in Paris in a European Nations Cup qualifying game but from then on Ramsey began to build the kind of team he wanted.

He was never afraid to change it. The World Cup finals were well under way when, having previously placed much emphasis on wingers, he decided that the ones he had were not working and dropped them, deploying instead a 4-4-2 system which would be deemed his 'wingless wonders'. Some felt the strategy, though it won the World Cup, did great harm to English football through its imitators in the years to come. The decision to drop Jimmy Greaves, the finest inside-forward of his time and most prolific scorer, also caused great controversy.

But criticism never overtly bothered Ramsey. His loyalty to his team was absolute, his contempt for the press scarcely dissembled. Football, he said, was something he deemed immensely important. Those who had not played it at a professional level were plainly beyond the pale.

West Germany's late, somewhat fortuitous, equaliser for 2-2 in the World Cup final at Wembley saw Ramsey at his most inspirational. Two days earlier, when his squad trained at Roehampton and he made the decision to omit Greaves, he was asked whether he still thought England would win the World Cup. There was a strangulated pause until at last he answered, 'Yes.'

As his disappointed, wearied England players sprawled about the turf before extra-time Ramsey told them: 'You've won it once. Now you must win it again.' With the help of Geoff Hurst's cross-bar-hitting, controversial goal for 3-2 they did, Hurst completing his hat-trick just before the end. After which little Nobby Stiles, kept in the team by Ramsey despite official displeasure from the Football Association after he had fouled Jacky Simon, of France, in a group game in front of the royal box, cried: 'You did it, Alf! We'd have been nothing without you.'

Ramsey had an excellent team to defend the trophy in Mexico in 1970 and might have gone beyond the quarter-finals had Gordon Banks, a superb goalkeeper, not suffered food poisoning and been ruled out of that crucial game, which in the end was lost to West Germany in Leon after England had led 2-0.

Throughout the tournament Ramsey was plagued by echoes of comments he had made in the 1966 tournament after a bruising match against Argentina in the quarter-finals. The Argentinian players had virtually run riot after the game and an incensed Ramsey had said he hoped, in the semi-final, against Portugal, England would meet a team that wanted to play football 'and not act as animals'.

In later years he seemed to lose his touch. Crucial games were lost and he was forced out of his England job – before his contract ended – in 1974. It was a sad anticlimax and there was another when he unsuccessfully went back into club management with Birmingham City. He seemed by then to have mislaid his essential rapport with players and he retired to Ipswich, where he lived a reclusive life with occasional forays into journalism.

Knighted in 1967, he married Vickie Answorth in 1951. She and their adopted daughter, Tania, survive him.

Sir Alfred Ernest Ramsey, born January 22 1920 died April 28 1999

APRIL 18 2001

Arms and the slope

ALEC STOCK

Alec Stock's football career, first as player, mostly as manager, will be remembered above all for four things: his success with non-League Yeovil Town, which put mighty Sunderland out of the 1949 FA Cup; his fruitful, resourceful years as Leyton Orient's manager; his brief, unhappy interlude as assistant manager of Arsenal; and his almost equally brief spell as AS Roma's manager.

Stock was a miner's son, born in Peasedown St John, in the Somerset coalfields. After the General Strike his family moved to Dartford, in Kent. At school he became a promising rugby fly-half, playing soccer in the evenings. When he left school, he worked in a bank, which he detested. Soccer, as an amateur centre-forward, and cricket were a consolation. Jimmy Seed, Charlton's manager, saw him score a hat-trick in a trial at Tottenham and signed him.

The year was 1936. In 1938, without having had a first-team game, Stock moved across London to Queens Park Rangers, a club he was destined to manage, but an ankle injury hampered his career. When war broke out he joined an infantry regiment in which he was commissioned. When it became an armoured regiment, he was promoted to captain, commanding a tank, in which he was wounded in the 1944 battle for Caen. He was sent back to Wales to convalesce.

His ambition was to become a bookmaker but his wife, whom he married in 1943, persuaded him to answer Yeovil's advertisement for a manager and a shortage of personnel even persuaded him to play again, now as an inside-forward on the club's notorious sloping pitch.

Yeovil's total wage bill then was £80 a week but early in 1949, at home to Bury, they knocked the Second Division club out of the Cup. Then it was Sunderland, with such stars as Len Shackleton, and Stock scored the first goal in a remarkable 2-1 win, although he would later say the 3-1 win over Bury had given him more satisfaction. Reality intervened when, away from their slope in the next round, they lost 8-0 to Manchester United.

The ebullient little East End shoe manufacturer, Harry Zussman, then took him to Leyton Orient for what was a memorable partnership. Twice Stock left, twice Zussman would get him back as Stock patiently rebuilt the struggling Third Division South club. He signed and developed local amateurs such as Vic Groves and Stan Charlton, who were profitably sold to Arsenal. Twice Orient went all the way to the quarter-finals of the Cup, losing in 1952 to Arsenal.

Stock's tactics were pragmatic and intelligent. A policy of 20-yard passes was followed by one of tight defence, no square balls and reliance on the zip of the inside-forwards.

'I hate yes men,' said Stock in 1956, shortly before joining Arsenal. 'I love the boy who comes in and tells me he thinks I'm wrong. He's a man.' At Highbury that did not quite work out. The idea was that Stock would prop up and perhaps succeed Tom

Whittaker, pre-war trainer and post-war manager of the Gunners, whose team had fallen on mediocre times. Perhaps Stock over-compensated, addressing the Arsenal players aggressively, telling them that 20 of them would be sold. On one occasion he told a younger player, Danny Clapton, to go over to two seniors, the goal-keeper Jack Kelsey and captain Dennis Evans, with an ashtray and tell them to stub out their cigarettes. The players tapped their ash into the ashtray and went on smoking. It was over in 53 days.

Soon, to Zussman's delight, Stock was back at Orient but the following year he was off again. Gigi Peronace, the Calabrian foot-ball agent who had just brought off the coup of taking John Charles from Leeds United to Juventus, convinced Roma that Stock was their man. After a tug-of-war with Zussman Roma got their way.

But Stock's task in Rome was overshadowed from the first. Roma had appointed as senior executive Toni Busini, previously a joint selector of the Italian national team and a notorious intriguer.

Stock, never at ease under pressure and at the worst times afflicted by asthma, perhaps intentionally signed his own death warrant: he missed the train to Naples for an away match, so Busini and other officials picked the team and presented him with it as a *fait accompli*. He refused to sit on the managers' bench and was sacked the same evening.

Back he went to Leyton Orient and Zussman but then on to QPR (1959-68), Luton Town (1968-72) and Fulham (1972-76), whom he memorably took to the 1975 FA Cup final, where they lost 2-0 to West Ham. At QPR, with whom he won the League Cup in 1967, he worked harmoniously with a talented coach in Bill Dodgin Jr – 'Bill's got that lovely load of white hair,' he would say – though his contribution at training sessions tended to be marginal. 'We'd let him take it for a while,' said Dodgin. 'Then he'd throw down the whistle and go.'

But Stock was a man always highly estimated by his fellow

managers. His wife, Marjorie, died in 1986 and he is survived by his two daughters.

Alec William Alfred Stock, born March 30 1917, died April 16 2001

Trilby triumph

BOB STOKOE

Think of Bob Stokoe, who has died aged 73, and an indelible image comes to mind. It is Wembley in May 1973. Against all odds and expectations Second Divison Sunderland have just beaten mighty Leeds United 1-0 in the FA Cup final and on to the pitch, overcome by irrepressible joy, runs Stokoe, in his familiar trilby hat. He had many satisfactions in his long career as the Newcastle United centre-half, and manager of a string of clubs, but this surely was the high point.

Stokoe was born at Mickley, Northumberland, and joined nearby Newcastle. He made his debut as a centre-forward against Middlesbrough as an emergency choice on Christmas Day 1950. Standing just under 6ft and weighing just over 11st, he was no giant but prevailed with his quick anticipation and prowess in the air. Altogether he made 288 appearances for Newcastle. For a time he was switched to right-half but it was at centre-half that he won an FA Cup medal of his own, when, having succeeded the big Scottish international Frank Brennan in that role, he was a member of the Newcastle team that beat Manchester City 3-1 in 1955.

After that Stokoe had a spell with Hartlepools United before beginning his long managerial career at Bury. He stayed there from 1961 to 1965, scorning, as he once revealed, the offer of a bribe from Don Revie, then Leeds United manager, to lose a match. He then went south to manage Charlton Athletic before the first of three spells in charge of Carlisle United, culminating in 1986. Before he went to Sunderland, in 1972, he had success with Blackpool, who appointed him in 1970: he took them to two Anglo-Italian Cup finals in which they beat Bologna 2-1 in 1971 and lost to Roma 3-1 in 1972.

Sunderland's victory in that 1973 Cup final made them the first Second Division team to win the trophy since West Bromwich Albion in 1931 but their achievement was much the more remarkable. Not only were they facing a Leeds team that had dominated English football with its international stars but, where West Bromwich had been about to rejoin the First Division, Sunderland rose to victory from deep in the Second Division with a team that could not boast a cap between them. It was their first FA Cup triumph since 1937, when they beat Preston North End.

One irony of the match was that the Sunderland goalkeeper, Jim Montgomery, who could seldom have handled the ball so ineptly, was destined to make one of the finest saves seen in a Cup final when a ferocious shot, close in, from the formidable right foot of the Scottish international right-winger Peter Lorimer was somehow turned on to the Sunderland bar.

Territorially, and perhaps inevitably, Leeds had much the better of the exchanges but it was to Stokoe's credit that Sunderland showed uncompromising grit. Oddly what seemed an error by little Bobby Kerr, the Sunderland midfielder, led to the goal. Electing to shoot from 30 yards, when a pass to the unmarked Vic Halom on his right looked a better option, he saw the Leeds keeper, David Harvey, cautiously turn the ball over the bar. Billy

Hughes took the corner, Halom flicked the ball on and, with the Leeds defence in confusion, Ian Porterfield calmly brought it down and scored with his supposedly weaker right foot.

In the 1975-76 season Stokoe guided Sunderland back to the First Division before embarking on a round trip of former managerial posts that took in Bury, Blackpool, Rochdale and Carlisle before a brief reappearance as caretaker at Roker Park in 1987.

In later years he suffered from senile dementia. His wife, Joan, predeceased him.

Robert Stokoe, born September 21 1930, died February 1 2004

FEBRUARY 18 2002

Talking head

SIR WALTER WINTERBOTTOM

Sir Walter Winterbottom, who has died aged 88, was the first full-time manager of the England football team and kept the job for an astonishing 16 years, from 1946 to 1962. During this time England consistently qualified for the World Cup, although in the 1950 tournament in Brazil they lost 1-0 to the United States, possibly the greatest humiliation in the history of English football.

Winterbottom was concurrently director of coaching at the Football Association and was wont to say that he considered this the more important of his jobs. When his mentor, the FA secretary, Sir Stanley Rous, retired in 1962, everyone expected Winterbottom to succeed him. But Professor Sir Harold Thompson, who detested Rous and was later to progress up the hierarchy to chairman, succeeded in steering through a compromise candidate and

Winterbottom instead became secretary of the Central Council of Physical Recreation. He was knighted in 1978.

The charge that Winterbottom could not communicate with England players because he had not played professional football himself was unfair. He had in fact played it with some success. Born in Lancashire, he was educated at Oldham Grammar School and Chester College. It was there that he met Eddie Lever, a Portsmouth footballer whose career had just been ended by a knee injury. In later years Lever would become Portsmouth's manager. Long conversations about tactics stimulated the young Winterbottom. 'It was largely from Eddie Lever's knowledge,' he admitted, 'that I got my yearning for the game.'

Winterbottom then became a schoolmaster. He taught for three years in Oldham, playing centre-half meanwhile for Royton Amateurs in the Lancashire and Cheshire League, and for Mossley. It was here that he was spotted by Manchester United's legendary chief scout, Louis Rocca, and the money he earned from turning professional with United allowed him to study at Carnegie Physical Training College, where eventually he joined the staff.

His debut for United was in 1934, in a league match versus Leeds, which he remembered chiefly because he had eaten something that upset him and he felt violently ill. Yet he played well enough to displace, for a time, one of United's salient pre-war players, George Vose. Spinal trouble put him prematurely out of the game, though, and in 1939 he joined the RAF, becoming chief instructor of physical training at RAF Cosford, then head of physical training at the Air Ministry. He later resumed his playing career, turning out as a guest for Chelsea at half-back and full-back, and was even named twice as an England reserve. A star he may not have been but he had every right to call himself a first-class footballer.

When he was appointed England manager and senior FA coach in 1946 he inaugurated a series of courses. He was concurrently in charge of the senior, amateur and youth international teams – the latter two a new departure – till pressure of work obliged him to give up the last two responsibilities.

He found himself confronted by a welter of prejudice and ignorance. If the FA coaching scheme may in later years have ossified into a new orthodoxy, initially it had much to offer and much to contend with. At many clubs training still consisted of endless running round the track, with nothing seen of the ball, the theory being that the less players saw of it during the week, the more they would want it on a Saturday.

Having never been a club manager, Winterbottom found himself subject to much criticism. And so he gathered around him a band of like-minded disciples, men such as Ron Greenwood and Bill Nicholson, who would become influential managers in the years to come. Tall, agile, pipe-smoking and bespectacled, he could have passed for a public school beak, which had much to do with the way he was perceived. Coaching, he insisted, was merely 'a means of showing how to practise'. His apophthegms were always illuminating: 'Football is a game where superiority in match play can't always be indicated by goals, because of the difficulty of scoring.'

He inherited a talented England team, though he never, officially, had responsibility for picking it. He deferred in this to a panel of selectors and yet he was the target for criticism when things went wrong. However, by the 1958 World Cup finals, England's third in a row, he had the selectors dancing to his tune.

In no other footballing country in the world could a manager with Winterbottom's results have survived so long. You could hardly blame him for the ghastly defeat in Brazil when, as he said, 'We did have our chances, dozens of them,' but he was never an inspirational figure, he had a tendency to talk above his players' heads and, for all his interest in tactics, his strategies were often flawed.

This became particularly plain in 1953, when England were thrashed 6-3 by Hungary at Wembley. When they went to Budapest the following May they had learned so little they were humiliated 7-1. Still Winterbottom kept his job and took the team on to the 1954 World Cup in Switzerland, where they honourably attained the quarter-finals.

Meanwhile the FA coaching scheme was becoming the domain of theorist schoolmasters who, unlike Winterbottom, had never played at professional level. Jargon abounded. Asked once about the ability of certain players almost to photograph the field around them, Winterbottom replied, 'We know all about that but we call it environmental awareness.'

England's 1958 prospects were damaged by the Munich air crash, which killed three key players – Roger Byrne, Tommy Taylor and Duncan Edwards. But leaving the Bolton centre-forward Nat Lofthouse out of the World Cup party was an evident blunder. A second was not to give the young Bobby Charlton a single World Cup game. A third was to throw two neophytes, Peter Broadbent and Peter Brabrook, in at the deep end for the doomed play-off against the Soviet Union.

But under Winterbottom England qualified again in 1962 and reached the quarter-finals, going out to Brazil. The time had come, it seemed, for Winterbottom to succeed Rous – which he would have done but for the machinations of Harold Thompson.

He married his wife, Ann, in 1942. She and their two daughters survive him. A son predeceased him.

Sir Walter Winterbottom, born March 31 1913, died February 16 2002

ABOUT THE AUTHOR

Brian Glanville has written a number of sports articles for the *Guardian*. He is author of *Football Memories* (1999), *The Story of the World Cup: The Essential Companion to Germany 2006* (2006) and *England Managers: The Toughest Job in Football* (2008).